D1502972

Presented to:

_____

From:

_____

Date:

_____

Honor Books® is an imprint of
Cook Communications Ministries, Colorado Springs, Colorado 80918
Cook Communications, Paris, Ontario
Kingsway Communications Ltd, Eastbourne, England

*The Wonder of Christmas*
*Celebrating the True Spirit of the Season*
© 2005 by Derric Johnson

First printing, 2005
Printed in Canada.
3 4 5 6 Printing/Year 09 08 07 06

Developed by Bordon Books

Scripture quotations marked NIV are taken from the *Holy Bible, New
International Version* ®. NIV ®. Copyright © 1973, 1978, 1984 by
International Bible Society. Used by permission of Zondervan Publishing
House. All rights reserved; NKJV are taken from *The New King James Version.*
Copyright © 1979, 1980, 1982, Thomas Nelson, Inc.; TLB are taken from
*The Living Bible* © 1971. Used by permission of Tyndale House Publishers,
Inc., Wheaton, Illinois 60189. All rights reserved; KJV are taken from the
*King James Version of the Bible.*

ISBN 1-56292-532-6

# The Wonder of Christmas

Celebrating the True Spirit of the Season

by Derric Johnson

# The Wonder of Christmas

## Celebrating the True Spirit of the Season

by Derric Johnson

HONOR **HB** BOOKS

*Inspiration and Motivation for the Seasons of Life*
An Imprint of Cook Communications Ministries • Colorado Springs, Colorado

# Contents

# Dedication

When God sent His Son
into this world two thousand years ago
for that first Christmas party in Bethlehem,
He was showing His deep love for all mankind.

When His Son died on the cross for our sins,
He was demonstrating the greatness of His love
for a wounded world.

When Jesus rose from the grave ...
proving that we could do that too ...
that was enough illustrated love.

But ... if He ever wanted to do anything
more to prove His love for me,
He did it when He gave me Debbie,
the most wonderful wife and partner
anyone could ever hope for.

She creates a constant Christmas.
It's like Jesus is born all over again every day
in her serene spirit,
beautiful countenance,
and joyous life.

So it's easy to dedicate this book to
my wife, Debbie,
who makes life meaningful, vibrant,
worthwhile, and necessary.

# Introduction

Christmas is ... not Christmas was.

Christmas is ... as present as the air we breathe,

    as current as the events that please or perplex us.

Christmas is ... light.

    More than the light from a new star ...

    it's the light of God's eternal love

    shining through the midnight of man's despair,

    proving that He believed in man.

Christmas is ... giving.

    Not of wise men to God,

    but of God to men who would be

    wise enough to receive the gift of His Son.

Christmas is ... joy.

    Not just because man heard a new song,

    but because God wrote it and had it sung.

Christmas is ... the angel saying, " ... to all people."

    And that means everybody ...

    everywhere ...

    and that includes you!

# The Wonder of Christmas Is ...

## MUSIC

If the words tell us how to believe,
then the music tells us how to feel.

# FOURTEEN WORDS

*A*s the bright copper penny of the sun slid down into the blue velvet pocket of night, nothing was changed. It had been a day like all the rest. Another 24-hour carbon copy etched in despair and outlined with discouragement.
It was an unhappy, suspicious, fearful, needy world into which Jesus came.
A world of moral degradation,
low ethical standards,
and bitter hatred.
Sounds familiar, doesn't it?
Government oppression was intolerable.
Taxes were rising at such alarming rates
that personal needs could scarcely be met.
Religious vitality was at an all-time low.
People had lost purpose ...
and hope ...
and faith.
Still sounds familiar, doesn't it?
The darkness of that night was matched only by the gloom of
the spirit that pervaded the countryside.
But God surprised the world with a simple song ...

GLORY TO GOD IN THE HIGHEST,
AND ON EARTH PEACE,
GOOD WILL TOWARD MEN.

Fourteen words ... that's all ... just 14 words!  Complex enough to keep theologians and philosophers pondering for twenty centuries, yet simple enough for a child to understand.

GLORY TO GOD IN THE HIGHEST,
AND ON EARTH PEACE,
GOOD WILL TOWARD MEN.

A song sent from heaven, brought by angels to touch the hurting heart of man.  And even today, if you listen carefully, you can still hear the angels sing.

For the common things of every day,
God gave man speech in the common way;

For the deeper things men think and feel,
God gave poets words to reveal;

But for the heights and depths no words can reach,
God gave man music, the soul's own speech.

# THE ORGAN WAS BROKEN

If the church organ had not broken down, and if the organist had not been able to strum a few chords on the guitar, then the loveliest Christmas carol of them all would never have been written.

Joseph was a twenty-six-year-old German priest when his organist told him that the pipe organ could not be used that night for the traditional Christmas Eve service. Franz was well trained in his instrument, but he just didn't have the time or the parts to make the necessary repairs in one afternoon.

So to relieve his disappointment, Joseph went out visiting people in his parish. Shortly after arriving in one home, a new baby was born, and in his mind, the pastor compared that event with the birth of the Christ child centuries earlier. Walking home through the snow, Father Joseph envisioned a poem about that first Christmas. He hurriedly jotted down four stanzas and gave it to Franz.

While the organist read the words, the priest picked up a guitar and handed it to him, saying, "If we can't have the old organ, at least we can have a new song. Try your hand at this."

"But I know only three chords," Franz protested.

"Well then, write a song with those chords," Joseph insisted.

To quiet his friend, Franz strummed a few simple chords on the guitar. Soon he was humming an original melody.

And at midnight, the new carol was sung for the first time.

Because the old organ didn't work, two men did—Joseph Mohr and Franz Gruber.  They combined the poetry and music of their hearts and gave the world STILLE NACHT, or as you know it today, SILENT NIGHT.

Silent night, holy night,
All is calm, all is bright,
Round yon Virgin Mother and Child.
Holy Infant so tender and mild,
Sleep in Heavenly Peace,
Sleep in Heavenly Peace.

# THE WISE MEN AND MARY'S SONG

The kings who went to see the baby Jesus in Bethlehem were Magi, a religious caste among the Persians. Their dedication to astrology, divination, and the interpretation of dreams led them on a journey into historic memory.

We all know the Magi took three gifts to the baby Jesus in Bethlehem. An old legend describes the coming of the offering bearers this way:

One of the gift presenters was a young man, Caspar. In his youthful idealism, he was looking for a king, someone who could be a leader of regal stature with far-reaching influence and power. He carried with him gold, the most precious metal known to man, so elegant that only the rich could afford it and so rare that poor people had no use for it. That was to be his fitting gift for someone of promised royalty.

Another, Melchior, was middle-aged, and to satisfy the deep questions that disturbed his maturing mind, he yearned to find a God who could define purpose and value for his life. His gift was frankincense, a perfumed incense used in temple worship. As the smoke of the incense rose, it carried the prayers of the righteous with it toward heaven.

The third king was Balthazar, an elder statesman, getting up in age with many sin-stained years behind him. He longed to discover a Savior. In his mind, he felt that a Redeemer would have to suffer, so he took with him a gift of sweet-smelling myrrh, an aromatic gum used as a spice in burials.

In Bethlehem, the legend says, they listened to the song of Mary:

"My soul doth magnify the Lord ..."

Caspar cried out, "I have found my Lord, my Sovereign, my King." And he fell down and worshiped.

"And my spirit hath rejoiced in God ..."

"I have found my God, for whom I have searched near and far," exclaimed Melchior as he knelt reverently.

"In God my Savior ..."

"Here at last there is salvation for me. After all these years I have found my Messiah," Balthazar whispered. He, too, bent to adore and worship the young child.

Had they been singers, they would have joined the angels in singing, "Glory to God in the highest, and on earth peace, good will toward men."

# THE PERFECT MARRIAGE

Johann was born in 1397. Charles came into this world in 1707, and Felix began his life in 1809. So what binds these three men of four centuries together?

Well, it happened this way: In 1440, Johann Gutenberg invented the printing press, a machine that changed world history. To honor that invention on its 400th anniversary, Felix Mendelssohn was commissioned to compose special music to be played during a gigantic civic celebration.

The music did not have any lasting impact, but Felix shared with his publisher that he felt one of those melodies could have life beyond the presentation. "But," he hastened to add, "this melody should never be married to a religious text. It will never go with sacred words."

A century earlier Charles Wesley, the poet of the burgeoning Methodist Church which had been founded by his brother, John, was writing hymn poems every week. When he finished his life, more than 6,000 hymn texts had flowed from his pen.

One of his favorite hymns was a Christmas carol. But no one had ever found a suitable musical setting for his brilliant words. The song languished for years, bouncing between melodies, none of which matched the grandeur of the poem.

Then in 1855, William Cummings took Felix's "Ode To Ink" melody and married it to Charles' verses. That combination has clicked for over a century and a half now, appearing in nearly every church hymnal and on most

Christmas albums.

Never be married to a religious text because the two would be totally incompatible?

Hey, Felix. Surprise!

> Hark! The herald angels sing,
> "Glory to the newborn King;
> Peace on earth and mercy mild,
> God and sinners reconciled!"
> Joyful, all ye nations rise,
> Join the triumph of the skies,
> With th' angelic host proclaim,
> "Christ is born in Bethlehem."
> Hark! the herald angels sing,
> "Glory to the newborn King!"

# THE REAL MEANING

In 1692, eighteen-year-old Isaac complained about the awkward psalm-singing at their church. His father replied, "Then give us something better to sing, young man." And Isaac did.

He was born in Southampton, England, where his father was a deacon in the Congregational Church. When he was a baby, Isaac visited the local prison many times in his mother's arms as she saw her husband, who was jailed for his dissenter beliefs. That helps explain Isaac's staunch theological position throughout his life.

Isaac Watts is called "the father of English hymnody." In 1707, he published a collection of 210 of his own hymns, the first real hymnbook in the English language. Prior to that historic volume, churches had believed that only translations and adaptations of the book of Psalms were acceptable as hymns.

He was ordained as a clergyman of the Reformed Church and received recognition and acclaim as a scholar. His published work entitled *Logic* was long used as a textbook at Oxford while, in contrast, his nursery rhymes and books for children were widely read until the early 1900s.

Always frail in health, he never married but was content to give himself to his writing.

Among all of his famous hymn poems, there is only one memorable Christmas carol. But, ironically, Isaac never intended for "Joy to the World" to be sung only during the

Christmas season.  He intended it to be a carol chronicling Christ's second advent—not His first.  Pay attention to these words.

> Joy to the world!  The Lord is come,
> Let earth receive her King;
> Let every heart prepare Him room,
> And heaven and nature sing.
>
> Joy to the world!  The Savior reigns,
> Let men their songs employ;
> While fields and floods, rocks, hills, and plains,
> Repeat their sounding joy.
>
> No more let sin and sorrow grow,
> Nor thorns infest the ground;
> He comes to make His blessings flow
> Far as the curse is found.
>
> He rules the world with truth and grace,
> And makes the nations prove
> The glories of His righteousness,
> And wonders of His love.

# CHRISTMAS BELLS

I heard the bells on Christmas Day
Their old, familiar carols play,
And wild and sweet
The words repeat
Of peace on earth, good-will to men!

I thought how, as the day had come,
The belfries of all Christendom
Had rolled along
The unbroken song
Of peace on earth, good-will to men!

Till, ringing, singing on its way
The world revolved from night to day,
A voice, a chime,
A chant sublime
Of peace on earth, good-will to men!

Then from each black, accursed mouth
The cannon thundered in the South,
And with the sound
The Carols drowned
Of peace on earth, good-will to men!

And in despair I bowed my head;
"There is no peace on earth," I said;

"For hate is strong
And mocks the song
Of peace on earth, good-will to men!"

Then pealed the bells more loud and deep:
"God is not dead; nor doth he sleep!
The Wrong shall fail,
The Right prevail
With peace on earth, good-will to men!"

—HENRY WADSWORTH LONGFELLOW

✳

# FRACTURED CHRISTMAS CAROLS

Sing Along with These New Takes on Old Favorites:

- Deck the halls with Buddy Holly
- We three kings of porridge and tar
- On the first day of Christmas my tulip gave to me
- Later on we'll perspire, as we dream by the fire
- He's making a list, chicken and rice
- Noel, Noel. Barney's the King of Israel
- With the jelly host proclaim
- Olive, the other reindeer
- Frosty, the Snowman, is a ferret elf, I say
- Sleep in heavenly peas
- You'll go down in Listerine
- Oh, what fun it is to ride with one horse, soap, and hay
- Come, froggy faithful
- Good tidings we bring to you and your kid

# White Christmas

In 1939 Israel Baline composed a Christmas song, but he thought so little of it that he never showed it to anyone. He just tossed it into a trunk and didn't see fit to retrieve it until he needed it ten years later for a Bing Crosby-Fred Astaire movie, *Holiday Inn*.

Bing Crosby was a staunch Catholic, and at first he refused to sing the song because he felt it tended to commercialize Christmas. He finally agreed, took eighteen minutes to make the recording, and then the "throw away" song become an all-time hit.

Crosby's version has sold over 40 million copies. All together, this song has appeared in 750 versions, selling 6 million copies of sheet music and 90,000,000 recordings in the United States and Canada alone.

You might not recognize the song from the movie *Holiday Inn*, or from the composer, later known as Irving Berlin. But you're bound to know it, because it's on everyone's list of Christmas favorites—"I'm Dreaming of a White Christmas."

# STIMULATING SEASONAL SONGS FROM ROGET'S THESAURUS

Move hitherward the assembly of those who are loyal in their belief. —*O Come, All Ye Faithful*

Listen, the celestial messengers produce harmonious sounds. —*Hark! The Herald Angels Sing*

Nocturnal time span of unbroken quietness. —*Silent Night*

An emotion excited by the expectation of good given to this sphere. —*Joy to the World*

Embellish the interior passageways. —*Deck the Halls*

Exalted heavenly beings to whom mankind harkened. —*Angels We Have Heard on High*

Twelve o'clock on a clement night witnessed its arrival. —*It Came upon the Midnight Clear*

The Christmas preceding all others. —*The First Noel*

Small municipality in Judea southeast of Jerusalem. —*O Little Town of Bethleham*

Diminutive master of skin-covered percussionistic cylinders. —*The Little Drummer Boy*

Supreme being who elicits respite to ecstatic distinguished males. —*God Rest Ye, Merry Gentlemen*

In awe of the nocturnal time span characterized by religiosity. —*O Holy Night*

Geographic state of fantasy during Mother Nature's dormancy. —*Winter Wonderland*

Tintinnabulation of vacillating pendulums in resonant cups. —*Carol of the Bells*

Proceed declaring upon a specific geological alpine formation. —*Go Tell It on the Mountain*

# JUST ONE STAR

Back in the throne room of heaven, plans were being made to announce the birth of God's Son on earth. Michael, the archangel, had just finished describing his great heavenly display of comets and falling stars.

Gabriel went on with his musical plans—a great angelic choir of tens of thousands of voices, tuned with heaven's finest and latest harmonies, ready to serenade the earth.

But God interrupted their conversation. "No," He said, "that's not really what I had in mind. I planned a small family gathering in Bethlehem, actually. We don't need all those trimmings."

"But ... all my stars ... " said Michael. "What will I do with them?"

"And my music," Gabriel added.

Just then Jesus stepped through the pearly gates, out onto the red carpet of time, and started down the spiral stairway of stars.

Michael pleaded, "Father, let us do something, please! He simply can't go unannounced!"

"Well, all right," God said. "Gabriel, a few angels ... and, Michael, just one star."

# The Wonder of Christmas Is ...

## DELIGHT

Did you get everything
you wanted for Christmas?
*No ... but that's okay.*
*It wasn't my birthday party.*

# THE PROFESSOR TOLD A LIE

Clem grew up in a parsonage. His daddy was a preacher, then a bishop, and finally president of Columbia College. So you can understand how Clem skipped boyhood and became a scholar.

He was professor of Biblical Learning at General Theological Seminary where he authored *A Compendious Lexicon of the Hebrew Language*. Not exactly a best-seller.

In 1813 Professor Clem looked up from his reading and writing long enough to discover love. He got married, started a family, and began to explore the wonderland of make-believe.

And one day he authored a false statement. If he had told it only to his children, nothing would have happened, but the meticulous professor wrote it down.

A friend of the family saw a copy and sent it to a New York newspaper. The story was copied ... repeatedly.

Thousands came to believe it, and all Clem could do was hope no one ever discovered that he, the distinguished professor of languages, had written this unmitigated falsehood based on the appearance and manner of an old German handyman who worked around the professorial house.

Finally, 15 years after it was first published, with his children grown and gone, he confessed. And the whole world rose up to thank him.

Forgotten is his *Compendious Lexicon*. We remember Dr.

Clement Clarks Moore for the one whimsical verse which embarrassed him, and began ... "'Twas the night before Christmas ..."

'Twas the night before Christmas, and all through the house
Not a creature was stirring, not even a mouse.
The stockings were hung by the chimney with care ...
We'd worn them all week, and they needed the air.

## THE THREE STAGES OF MAN

1. He believes in Santa Claus
2. He doesn't believe in Santa Claus
3. He IS Santa Claus.

# THE TWELVE DAYS AFTER CHRISTMAS

*T*he first day after Christmas,
my true love and I had a fight.
And so I chopped the pear tree down,
and burned it just for spite.
Then with a single cartridge, I shot that blasted partridge ...
My true love gave to me.

The second day after Christmas,
I pulled on my old rubber gloves
And very gently wrung the necks of both the turtle doves ...
My true love gave to me.

The third day after Christmas, my mother caught the croup;
I had to use the three French hens to
make some chicken soup.
The four calling birds were a big mistake,
for their language was obscene.
The five gold rings were completely fake,
and they turned my fingers green.

The sixth day after Christmas,
the six laying geese wouldn't lay;
So I gave the whole worthless gaggle to the ASPCA.
On the seventh day, what a mess I found:

All seven of the swimming swans had drowned ...
That my true love gave to me.
The eighth day after Christmas, before they could suspect,
I bundled up the eight maids a-milking,
the nine pipers piping,
The ten ladies dancing, the eleven lords a-leaping
And the twelve drummers drumming,
and sent them back collect.

I wrote my true love, "We are through, love,"
And I said in so many words,
"Furthermore, your Christmas gifts were really for the birds
... Four calling birds,
Three French hens,
Two turtle doves
And a partridge in a pear tree."

The three saddest words on Christmas morning are:
"Batteries not included"
unless you're a parent, in which case they are:
"Some assembly required."

# CHRISTMAS ANAGRAMS

Each phrase below is an anagram of the title of a song, a film, or a story with a Christmas theme. The phrases are also clues, loosely speaking, to the titles from which they were created. For example, if "Chestnuts Roasting on an Open Fire" were the song title, its letters might be rearranged to appear in this list as "Fun nite persons eating hot acorns." Ignore all punctuation in the anagrams, and add any needed punctuation to your answers.

1. CHEF MOTHER, I MISS ALL… ROB

2. FELLOW IS A TRUE FIND

3. FOREMOST CHILDHOOD WAR SEEN

4. NOEL HERO STIRRED UP HERDED DEN

5. NOSTALGIC SNOWSUIT-COAT MAN

6. TRY LOUD TIMBREL THEME

7. WHY THAT REVEL?  SCADS OF ITEMS!

8. YON WARMTH SOFTENS

1. "I'll Be Home for Christmas"   2. "It's a Wonderful Life"   3. "March of the Wooden Soldiers"
4. "Rudolf, the Red-Nosed Reindeer"   5. "Santa Claus Is Coming to Town"   6. "The Little
Drummer Boy"   7. "The Twelve Days of Christmas"   8. "Frosty, the Snowman"

# THE HAPPY PARASITE

I t's hard to believe that anything which could bring so much joy is classified as a parasite. But it's true!

The technical name for this Christmas delight is literally "tree thief." But, of course, it's not all bad. Actually this fungus is good enough that Oklahoma made the decoration its official state flower.

To the early inhabitants of the British Isles, it was a magical plant and the object of worship. Some ancients wore it around the neck to ward off disease. Others stuck a sprig in their hats to guarantee good hunting.

The Japanese were convinced that it would increase crop growth and fertility. The Swiss shot it out of trees with arrows for good luck and happy days. Italian peasants thought the happy parasite offered protection against harm in general, and fire in particular. In old England, the first cow that produced a calf after New Year's Day was bedecked with a garland of its leaves.

Our early colonists kept sprigs of the plant under their pillow to induce dreams of happy days to come. Young girls believed they could receive a dream-preview of their future spouses.

You know what it is? Sure you do ... you've seen plenty of it ... every year. No one in America today expects it to drive away evil spirits or roll back prices or solve the energy crisis.

But it does enliven dull parties and offer hope to the kissless. It's mistletoe.

# SOLVING THE SEASON'S SORROWS

It is a fact that depression, often called the "common cold" of emotional problems, is intensified during the Christmas season. During this time of the year more than any other time, causes of depression are manifold:

- recent loss of loved ones through death or divorce,
- geographical separation of families,
- broken relationships,
- aloneness,
- reflections of past holidays.

These reasons generally cause people to become introspective and spend their time focusing on the past rather than on the present.

How then can we deal with depression during the holiday season? Try these suggestions...

1. DON'T BE IDLE. Do something kind for someone else. This takes your mind off yourself and focuses it on the needs of someone else.

2. DON'T LIVE IN THE PAST. We can control only the present, and our energies must be invested in doing something rewarding in the present without attention to the past.

3. BE KIND TO YOURSELF. Degrading yourself only intensifies depression.

4. PLAN SOME EXCITING ACTIVITY AFTER CHRISTMAS.

5. LISTEN TO UPLIFTING MUSIC. Music washes away

the dust of everyday life from the soul. Music serves as medicine to our emotions.

6. LEARN TO FORGIVE. The cloak of forgiveness cannot be worn over the coat of resentment. Most of us can forgive and forget. We just don't want the other person to forget that we forgave.

7. RENEW YOUR FAITH IN GOD. Remember that He gave the gift of His Son to us and use that as an example to be unselfish in what we do for others. Look around and notice the good things He has given you.

*L*ove makes our friends a little dearer,
Joy makes our hearts a little lighter,
Faith makes our paths a little clearer,
Hope makes our lives a little brighter,
Peace brings us all a little nearer.

## ALL I WANT FROM SANTA IS . . .

- for him to make my little sister disappear.
- more diapers for my baby brother. My mom says he's 90 percent liquid.
- a hundred-pound box of thousand-dollar bills.
- nothing selfish about me. I just want something plain and simple for my mother—a son-in-law!

## MURPHY'S LAW ... CHRISTMAS STYLE

The time it takes to find a parking place is inversely proportional to the amount of time you have to spend.

The more expensive a breakable gift is, the better the chances of dropping it.

The other line always moves faster.

Unassembled toys will have twice as many screws as you expect, and some will always be left over.

Interchangeable parts aren't.

All children have built-in detection devices when it comes to finding the Christmas gifts you've so cleverly hidden.

Amnesia strikes all family members when the Scotch tape and scissors are needed.

When a broken toy is demonstrated for the store manager, it works perfectly.

# "IS THERE A SANTA CLAUS?"

The most famous editorial ever written is the one entitled "Yes, Virginia, There Is a Santa Claus." It has been reproduced in every conceivable form, in every quarter of the globe, since it first appeared in the *New York Sun* in 1897.

The question was raised in a letter to the newspaper by 8-year-old Virginia O'Hanlon of New York City, the daughter of Dr. and Mrs. Phillip F. O'Hanlon. The classic answer was written by Frances Pharcellus Church, an editorial writer at The Sun.

Church took the assignment with reluctance, the story goes, but his fine craftsmanship produced an article that has endured and will continue to endure as long as children ask: "Is there a Santa Claus?"

We take pleasure in answering at once and thus prominently the communication below, expressing at the same time our great gratification that its faithful author is numbered among the friends of *The Sun:*

> *Dear Editor:*
> *I am 8 years old. Some of my little friends say there is no Santa Claus. Papa says, "If you see it in* The Sun *it's so." Please tell me the truth, is there a Santa Claus?*
> *Virginia O'Hanlon*
> *115 West 95th Street*

Virginia, your little friends are wrong. They have been affected by the skepticism of a skeptical age. They do not believe except what they see. They think that nothing can be which is not comprehensible by their little minds. All minds, Virginia, whether they be men's or children's, are little.

In this great universe of ours, man is a mere insect, an ant, in his intellect as compared with the boundless world about him, as measured by the intelligence capable of grasping the whole of truth and knowledge.

Yes, Virginia, there is a Santa Claus. He exists as certainly as love and generosity and devotion exist, and you know that they abound and give to your life its highest beauty and joy. Alas! how dreary would be the world if there were no Santa Claus! It would be as dreary as if there were no Virginias.

There would be no childlike faith then, no poetry, no romance to make tolerable this existence. We should have no enjoyment, except in sense and sight. The eternal light with which childhood fills the world would be extinguished.

Not believe in Santa Claus! You might as well not believe in fairies! You might get your papa to hire men to watch in all the chimneys on Christmas eve to catch Santa Claus, but even if you did not see Santa Claus coming down, what would that prove? Nobody sees Santa Claus, but that is no sign that there is no Santa Claus.

The most real things in the world are those that neither children nor men can see. Did you ever see fairies dancing on the lawn? Of course not, but that's no proof that they are not there. Nobody can conceive or imagine all the wonders there are unseen and unseeable in the world.

You tear apart the baby's rattle and see what makes the noise inside, but there is a veil covering the unseen world which not the strongest man, nor even the united strength of all the strongest men that ever lived could tear apart.

Only faith, poetry, love, romance, can push aside that curtain and view and picture the supernal beauty and glory beyond. Is it all real? Ah, Virginia, in all this world there is nothing else real and abiding.

No Santa Claus! Thank God! he lives and he lives forever. A thousand years from now, Virginia, nay, 10 times 10,000 years from now, he will continue to make glad the heart of childhood.

# THE OTHER CHRISTMAS STORY

And there were in the same country husbands and fathers keeping watch over their homes by night but going to work every morning to make lots of money.

And lo, the smooth-voiced TV announcer came upon them, and the glories of many fine possessions shone out at them, and they were sore afraid that they would never be able to buy all the things their families wanted.

And the TV announcer said unto them, "Fear not, for I bring unto you good tidings of great joy, which shall be to all fathers, mothers, children, and relatives.

"For unto you there is this day, in the city where our store is, a saviour, which is our credit manager.

"And this shall be a sign unto you. You shall find this wondrous one wrapped in red clothing, with a big stomach, and sporting white whiskers. We call him Santa Claus."

And suddenly there was with the TV announcer a multitude of TV actors, praising the store and saying, "Glory to Santa, and on earth, lots of presents for all."

And it came to pass as the TV actors faded away, the fathers and mothers said one to another, "Let us now go even unto this store which the TV announcer hath made known unto us."

And they came with haste, and found glittering wristwatches, fur coats, transistor radios, electric can openers, new dresses, and also the Wondrous One, dressed in red, sitting by the cash register, saying, "Ho, ho, ho."

And when they had made their purchases, they spoke now among all their neighbors how they were going to have one of the best Christmases ever, but Santa Claus kept all the time contracts in his safe and pondered on all the interest he was going to collect.

Be very careful that the message of what man has to sell does not overwhelm the proclamation of what God has to give.

What can I give Him,
Poor as I am?
If I were a shepherd,
I would bring a lamb.
If I were a Wise Man,
I would do my part,
Yet what can I give Him,
I give Him my heart.

CHRISTINA G. ROSSETTI

# The Wonder of Christmas Is...

TRUST

It's not so much that man could not
believe in God, but that God was proving
He believed in man.

## "CAN I HOLD YOUR BABY?"

In order to save the beautiful ceramic nativity set from the grasping, sticky fingers of her young daughter, Linda crafted a play grouping out of burlap, canvas, and yarn. Five-year-old Elizabeth would spend hours rearranging the pieces and acting out the Christmas story. Mother would quietly laugh to herself when she heard Elizabeth inevitably say, "Hey, Jesus' mother, can I hold your baby?"

Mother just couldn't picture the work-roughened hands of a shepherd cuddling an infant, or a royal king stooping down to embrace a poor child in a manger. But it made perfect sense to little Elizabeth; if these people were going to make a trip to see a baby, they wouldn't want to leave without holding it.

Think about it. She really isn't so far off. When you see any one of the newborn babies around your church, it's only natural to admire her or comment on how cute he is. But if you actually pick up that baby, a phenomenon takes place. Somehow, holding that child, gazing into those charming, wide eyes, and connecting with that uniquely God-given personality—that baby just gets into your heart!

Don't you think the shepherds and wise men were drawn in the same way to embrace the Infant of Bethlehem and experience the miracle of His love in their hearts that first Christmas?

As you make your journey to the stable in Bethlehem again this year, don't just gaze on the Child in the manger and turn away unchanged.  Embrace the Baby of Bethlehem, the pure light of God's love, and let Him shine in your hearts and make your lives new.

Don't leave without holding the baby.

*The Word became flesh and made his dwelling among us.*
*We have seen his glory, the glory of the One and Only,*
*who came from the Father, full of grace and truth.*

JOHN 1:14 NIV

## RISE UP, SHEPHERD

Imagine one of those shepherds from the first Christmas night. He was very young then, only a boy of seven. But now he's old, and his little grandson sits on his knee as he recounts that momentous evening.

"It was a long time ago, and I was just your age. Hard to believe I was ever as little as you, isn't it? Well ... we were on a hill, just outside of Bethlehem, watching over our flock of sheep, just like King David had done hundreds of years before, right in that same place.

"It always made me feel so grown-up when I got to stay out all night with my father. I really wanted to be a good shepherd someday, and this was the best way to start. The sheep were quiet and very still. I had almost fallen asleep when a great light shone around us. I thought at first it was a dream. But when I saw the angel and heard him speak, I knew it was real.

"The angel told us not to be afraid, because our Savior was born in Bethlehem. He said we should go and find Him, and he even gave us directions. My father and all my uncles and cousins wanted to go, but somebody had to stay with the sheep. They said they'd be right back.

"Bethlehem was very crowded that night, and there were lots of babies born. But only one was in a stable, lying in a manger wrapped up in swaddling clothes. Only one like that.

"When they got back a few hours later, they were all really

excited and told me all about it. I was really disappointed that I hadn't seen the baby on that first night, but I kept hearing about Him as He grew up. Everybody said He did astounding things—like healing the sick, making blind people see, and deaf people hear. Even raised some from the dead, they said.

"But then He got into some kind of trouble. There were some folks who didn't like Him. They killed Him by hanging Him on a cross. But I heard He didn't stay dead. A lot of people think He rose from the grave and really changed the world with hope and peace and love."

"Well, Grandpa, is it true?" his grandson asked. "Did all of that really happen?"

"That's the way I heard it," Grandpa replied.

"But is it really true?" the boy insisted.

Grandpa shook his head. "I don't know. I never went to see."

*Don't let that be your story. If you've only heard about it, you've missed the best part. It's not enough to know that Christmas comes to you; you have to come to Christmas.*

# IF ONLY ...

The entire Christmas story absolutely escaped George Albright. The whole "God born in a manger" thing was beyond him, or maybe it was just too simple for him to grasp. At least until last Christmas Eve when the snow began to fall.

He had just settled into his fireside chair and begun to read. There was a thumping sound on the window, and at first he thought someone was throwing snowballs. He went to the door and looked into the yard where he saw a small flock of birds huddled in the snow.

They'd been caught in the storm and then desperately tried to find shelter by flying through his large living room window. George knew he couldn't let those little creatures freeze, but how could he help them?

*The barn, of course,* he thought. *The barn where the children keep the pony will provide shelter, if I can get the birds in there.*

He opened the barn doors and turned on a light, but the birds didn't move.

Maybe some food would entice them. He sprinkled bread crumbs leading to the stable door. Nothing.

He tried catching them and shooing them in. The birds went everywhere except into the barn. They were afraid of him.

"I want them to trust me. How can I convince them I only want to help?"

But every move he made tended to frighten them more. They would not follow or be pushed.

*If only I could be a bird myself and mingle with them and speak their language and show them the way to the barn, then they could see and understand,* he thought.

Just then the church bells began to chime, "O Come, All Ye Faithful." Listening to the Good News, George understood and knelt in the snow with thankful belief.

The only blind person
at Christmastime
is he who has not
Christmas in his heart.

HELEN KELLER

# THE BETHLEHEM STAR

Soft winds are blowing
O'er Bethlehem's town,
Brightly the stars
From heaven look down.
Quietly the shepherds
Their long vigil keep
Over their flocks
Of slumbering sheep.
Hark!  There's a sound
On the pulsating air,
Music is stealing
From voices somewhere.
And a beautiful light
As a star settles down
O'er a stable that stands
At the edge of the town.

# THE STOLEN STATUE

In Los Angeles on Christmas morning twenty-five years ago, Father Hopkins unlocked the church doors in preparation for 6:00 A.M. mass. A quick perusal of the sanctuary showed everything in order. The worshipers came and went.

Then, just before the eight o'clock service, Father Hopkins checked around again, and to his great dismay, he noticed the Christ child was missing from the nativity scene. In the frantic search that followed, there was no sign of the statue. Everything else in the scene was untouched.

Strange that anyone would want this plaster-of-paris, hand-painted likeness of the baby Jesus. Complete, the manger set was not worth much; and alone, the one statue of the Child was worth less. But then, without the Son of God, the nativity scene was not worth anything at all.

The focal point was conspicuous by its absence. Who would do such a thing? Could it be pranksters, atheists, or maybe some Scrooge trying to spoil the happy, holy day?

No one was sure, but one fact was certain: Someone had walked into the chapel and stolen Christ right out of Christmas.

Then ... just before the nine o'clock service, a seven-year-old boy appeared at the front door of the church. He was pulling a brand-new wagon, and in the wagon was the missing statue.

"Juan, where did you find Jesus?" Father Hopkins asked.

"Oh, I didn't find Him; I took Him," the boy replied.

When asked why, he said, "Well, I prayed to Jesus for a new wagon, and I promised that when it came, I'd give Him the very first ride!"

*"Don't store up treasures here on earth*
*where they can erode away or may be stolen.*
*Store them in heaven where they will never*
*lose their value, and are safe from thieves.*
*If your profits are in heaven*
*your heart will be there too."*

MATTHEW 6:19-21 TLB

# THE PARADE OR THE MAIN EVENT

Nine-year-old Rusty had never seen a circus. When he heard one was coming to his Midwestern town, he worked feverishly to earn enough money to get in.

Finally, the big day arrived, and with ticket in hand, he rushed over to Main Street!

He carefully picked out a place along the curb and watched spellbound as the circus parade marched by.

The lions scared him, the elephants enthralled him, and the tumblers astounded him.

Then, adding to this enchantment, a silly clown with a sad face walked up to him and held out his baggy pockets as if bemoaning his poverty. Without a second thought, Rusty grinned and then dropped his ticket into the pocket and the clown was gone.

All too soon the rest of the parade passed by and Rusty ran all the way home. "Daddy! Daddy! The circus was wonderful!" And then he went on to describe his whole exciting experience.

His father realized what had taken place, and he wasn't sure how to break the news. He gently lifted his boy into his arms and said, "Rusty, I'm sorry. You didn't see the circus today—you only saw the parade."

"No, Daddy! I saw the circus!" the boy insisted.

"Sorry, Rusty, but you missed the main event. There's much more to the circus than just the parade."

Don't get caught up in the glitter and glamour of the tinsel and treasure. Christmas is all about Jesus coming to bring peace and love and hope into this world. The main thing is to keep the main thing, the main thing.

If Jesus were merely a man ... the cross was murder;
but if He was truly God ... it was an offering.
If Jesus were merely a man ... the cross was martyrdom;
but if He was truly God ... it was sacrifice.
If Jesus were merely a man ... they took His life;
but if He was truly God ... He laid it down willingly.
If Jesus were merely a man ... we are compelled
to admiration;
but if He was truly God ... we are compelled to adoration.
If Jesus were merely a man ... we need to stand and
take off our hats to Him;
but if He was truly God ... we need to bow and
give our lives to Him!

# LET ME BE THE MANGER

Joey was eight and he lived in an impoverished San Diego housing development. The church buses made periodic runs through his neighborhood to gather children for Sunday school and other special events.

The nice people invited him to a Christmas party. He would have 15 minutes to get dressed before the bus left for the church. Joey ran home and exploded with excitement to his mother, "There's a party at that big church this afternoon and I'm invited." He thought it was another "Halloween costume party." He and Mom went to work on his wardrobe. Fifteen minutes wasn't much time, and their funds were more limited than their minutes.

Mom had a great idea—why not go as a haystack? She put an old brown sweater on Joey and stuffed it with straw. They even put some of the weeds from a brook on the outside of the sweatshirt, just to make it look real.

But Joey was more than surprised when the party turned out to be a Christmas play instead of a costume party. He sulked around the fringes of the group until he heard the leaders say they couldn't find a manger.

"Can I help?" he asked. He was good at finding things. The parents explained to Joey that what they were looking for was a box full of hay where the baby Jesus could be laid. It seemed that someone had borrowed the prop. And how could they have an adequate Bethlehem drama without it?

Joey looked down at his costume—a baggy brown sweatshirt with weeds stuffed in it, and straw sticking out everywhere. "I could be a box of hay." He lay down on the floor and announced, "I'll be your manger. Let Jesus be born in me."

The way to Christmas lies
through an ancient gate. ...
It is a little gate,
child-high, child-wide,
and there is a password:
"Peace on earth to men of good will."
May you, this Christmas,
become as a little child again
and enter into His kingdom.

ANGELO PATRI

# The Wonder of Christmas Is...

## GIVING

The star still shines to make
every night a midnight clear.

# THE MOTHER GOD CHOSE

The mother God chose for the birth of His Son was an obscure peasant girl. Young, perhaps eighteen. To the people living closest to her, there was nothing to distinguish her from the other young ladies of her day. Yet God chose her to deliver His gift to the world. The angel said, "Hail, you that are highly favored, the Lord is with you: blessed are you among women. You will conceive in your womb and bring forth a son, and you shall call His name Jesus." (See Luke 1:28, 31.)

When Mary saw the angel, she was troubled in her heart and wondered what he meant.

That really was not the kind of favor she wanted from God. Think about it. Who would believe her? "Gabriel, are you going to tell this to my mother and father?"

"No."

"My friends in Nazareth?"

"No."

"Well, how about Joseph?"

"I ... could make a stop by his home. But remember, Mary, with God nothing shall be impossible!"

And God called it "favored."

Mary acquiesced. "Behold, the handmaid of the Lord. Be it unto me according to Thy word." (See Luke 1:38.)

A few days before the baby was born, she was required to take a long, painful journey to Bethlehem. When she got there, no one had bothered to make a reservation at the inn.

And even when new life stirred within her, only a dirty stable and the company of domestic animals were offered to her. There, in the bleak midwinter, she gave birth to the Son of God. And He called it "favored."

Then, because of the fear of Herod, Mary had to flee her homeland. Through the lands of the Philistines she traveled, and out across the measureless desert. You know she wanted to be with her people. But she cared for her baby, and as the angel said, she was "favored."

Finally, she returned with Joseph to their home in that little out-of-the-way village, Nazareth. In the words of Jesus, we catch a glimpse of the only home He ever knew. He recalled how one candle would light the entire house. How clothes were patched, and later patches were patched. Mary thrilled at her son's teaching, suffered at His death, rejoiced at His resurrection.

The angel said Mary gained the favor of God. She never doubted. And her faith gave us Jesus.

*H*e is greater than any ruler...
Mightier than any warrior...
Nobler than any king...
Wiser than any sage...
Bigger than any kingdom...
Better than any crown...
Lovelier than any name...
Worthy of our worship...
Deserving of our praise.

# THE FORGOTTEN FATHER

A worried mother phoned the church office on the afternoon of the Sunday school Christmas program. She was sorry to say that her son, who was playing the role of Joseph in the nativity scene, had a cold and was in bed on doctor's orders.

"Well, it's too late to get another Joseph now," the teacher replied. "We'll just write him out of the script." They did, and the sad thing is that no one missed him.

Joseph really is the forgotten man at the manger. I checked a well-known hymnbook which contains eleven Christmas carols, and not one reference to Joseph appears in their 41 verses. We sing of the Virgin Mother and Child, angels from the realms of glory, shepherds in the fields abiding, and three kings of the Orient. But we find nothing of Joseph.

Oh, I know he was a common man who didn't add much excitement to the story. And he never said a word that was recorded in Scripture. But we do know that he was a devout man. When he first heard that Mary was expecting a child, he was on his way to sever their engagement, with no thought of shaming her.

But when God revealed his eternal purpose, Joseph gladly became her husband, attended her at the hour of Christ's birth, arranged for the safety of the mother and child during the flight to Egypt, and later provided a home and companionship for Jesus.

By heritage Joseph was in the royal line of David. By vocation he was a carpenter. Matthew speaks of Joseph as being a just man, which in those days meant he lived in a right relationship with God. I guess the best word to describe Joseph, besides forgotten, is ordinary. And who cares about ordinary people ... except God?

Susan, four years old, engrossed in drawing a picture of the nativity scene, finally took it to her grandfather for his approval. "It's excellent, Susan," he said. "But why is one of Joseph's legs so much longer than the other?"

"Oh, he's stomping his foot," she explained. "He wanted a girl."

# 'TIS THE DAY AFTER CHRISTMAS

'Tis the day after Christmas, and out in the den
Daddy is watching pro football again.
The children are throwing and breaking their toys,
And Mother is up to her ears in the noise.

The melting snow drips through a hole in the roof;
Wow ... one of those reindeer sure had a sharp hoof.
Ribbons and wrappings are spread all around,
And we hope when they're cleared our lost boy will be found.

Santa long since disappeared in the fog,
The turkey is tasteless and the eggnog won't nog.
The holly and ivy, the tinsel and lights,
No longer bring warm glows on cold, darkened nights.

Children, who were last week helpful and sweet,
Have mouths that are sassy and rooms less than neat.
Those people with faces that smiled forth like elves,
Are now once again just their grouchy old selves.

Then carols of joy and hope filled the air,
But now they are muffled by hard rock's loud blare.
The cold winds which now make Aunt Josephine freeze,
Were not even noticed on Yule shopping sprees.

Why should such a great day let us down so hard?
Is there something about Christmas that we disregard?
The babe in the manger became a great man.
He grew up to be Savior. That was God's plan.

Remember when you take down that last Christmas bough,
He'll never love you more than He loves you right now.
And if we know that Christ loves us and always is near,
Then Christmas should be every day of the year.

# THE PRICE OF A MIRACLE

Sally was only eight years old, and it was a week before Christmas. The family had set out to do Christmas shopping, but when Kyle's lingering illness turned into something far more serious than they had ever imagined, they went by the emergency room, and then ended up at the neighborhood pharmacy instead. Kyle's heart was failing faster than expected. Sally tried to look brave standing outside Simpson's Drugstore with her worried mom and dad.

"Do you think this medicine will help little Kyle?" Daddy asked pensively.

"I don't know," Mommy answered. "At least these pills will keep him alive a little longer. He is so sick, and I think they've done everything they can to save his life."

"And we've done everything we can do too. If it's true that only a new heart can save him, that will take much more money than we have."

Sally heard Mommy say with whispered desperation, "Only a miracle can save him now." Sally reached deep into her coat pocket and gently fingered the money she had smuggled out of her piggy bank. It was all the money she had in the world—four dollars and eleven cents. It was supposed to buy nice Christmas presents for the family. But maybe her brother, Kyle, needed that money to help him get well.

Sally slipped back into the drugstore while her parents were still talking. She cleared her throat and shifted her weight back and forth to get the pharmacist's attention. "And what do you want?" he asked in an annoyed tone of voice. "I'm talking to my brother."

"Well, I want to talk to you about my brother. He's sick, and I want to buy a miracle."

"I beg your pardon."

"My Mommy says only a miracle can save him now, so how much does a miracle cost?"

"We don't sell miracles here, little girl. I can't help you."

"Listen," Sally insisted, "I have the money to pay for it. Just tell me how much it costs."

The pharmacist's brother, a well-dressed man, stooped down and asked, "What kind of a miracle do you need?"

"I don't know," Sally answered. A tear started to slide down her cheek. "I just know he's really sick, and Mommy says he needs an operation to get him a new heart. But my folks can't pay for it ... so I have my money. I want to buy the miracle that will get him a new heart."

"How much do you have?" the big man asked.

"Four dollars and eleven cents. And it's all the money I have in the whole world."

"Well, isn't that a coincidence?" he said, looking up at his brother. "Four dollars and eleven cents—that's the exact cost of a miracle to save a little brother."

He took her money in one hand, and with the other hand he grasped her mitten and said, "Take me to your parents. I want to meet them and see about saving your brother."

That well-dressed man was Dr. Carlton Armstrong, a renowned surgeon who specialized in pediatric heart transplants. In a few days, Kyle was in the hospital being prepared for surgery. Dr. Armstrong was talking with Sally during the few minutes' delay in moving her brother from his room to the operating room.

"We're going to give Kyle a new heart," he told her.

"What's wrong with the one he's got?" she asked.

"It's just not working correctly. His heart doesn't pump right, and frankly, it has some leaks. At his age, he should have a perfect heart."

"So, where do you find him another one? Is there a used-heart lot?"

"No. We get a heart from someone else."

"Wow! How do you pull that off or out?"

"Well, someone has to die in order for him to get a new heart. But it has to be someone really special. We can't use just any old heart. It has to be a perfect match for it to work. We found just the right one, and we're making the switch right away."

"Boy, if somebody gives him his heart—you know, trades his life for Kyle's—then Kyle better be worth it."

The operation was successfully completed without charge, and it wasn't long until Kyle was home again and doing well. Mommy and Daddy were happily talking about the chain of events that had led them to this place.

"That surgery," Mommy whispered. "It's like a miracle. I wonder how much it would have cost?" Sally smiled to herself. She knew exactly how much a miracle cost—four dollars and eleven cents, plus the faith of a little child.

# A GIFT IS NOT A GIFT

He comes with love
Which brings us hope
Which turns to joy
Which offers peace.
Little Baby tucked away
In a manger full of hay,
It's hard to believe what You are.
A gift from above,
The gift of God's love
Who was born long ago for today.
But a gift is not a gift until it is received,
And a truth is not a truth until it is believed.
Little Baby small and frail,
Whose birth today we hail,
It's hard to believe who You are.
If only You had been a carpenter born poor,
Who triumphed over life to become rich.
But instead You were a carpenter died poor,
That others like me might be rich.
But a gift is not a gift until it is received,
And a truth is not a truth until it is believed.
He comes with love
Which brings us hope
Which turns to joy
Which offers peace.

# GOD GAVE THE STAR

There will be little children on the hills of Bethlehem again this Christmas Eve, looking for The Star. There will be men and women all over the world, thinking how one night God hung a star from the floor of heaven to guide the humble and the wise. That Star will reflect "the hopes and fears of all the years," and man will take courage again and somehow go on.

God gave The Star. It has always been with us.

It got here at the dawn of creation when God said, "Let there be light," and, Job adds, "The morning stars broke forth in chorus."

It was hidden from us for a while, but it was born again into our world over a manger—a manger at Bethlehem.

It was a beautiful star, ready to give guidance to any man, woman, son, or daughter who cared to look at it.

But right from the start, some people just didn't like The Star.

They tried to ignore it. They said, "There's no Star. It simply doesn't exist."

Others tried to change its appearance.

Nations made laws to ban it.

Whole armies lined up to march against it.

They killed some who believed in The Star.

Scholars and philosophers screamed at it in fury. They tried to blot it out.

Finally, they nailed that Star to a tree.

And they said to themselves, "There! That should take care of that!"

But it didn't.

Laugh at it, sneer at it, deny it. Do anything you will with it. Yet here it is, the same tonight as it was in Herod's time. You cannot do one little thing to halt the nightly, majestic marching of God's stars across the skies. You can never do anything to dim the shining of His Star.

Believe this, and believe it well—only God could make a Star.

## STARS IN THE TREES

M artin was a preacher. Walking home one night after delivering a scathing sermon, attacking everything that he considered to be the enemies of Christ, a miraculous thing happened. He was a reformer and, some thought, a revolutionary. Most people regarded him as harsh and tough, highly focused, and overly obsessed with his doctrinal message.

But in reality, he was a family man, deeply dedicated to his wife, his six children (three boys and three girls), and his home. In fact, it was while he was walking back to his house that night when he paused for a moment of reverie.

Snow had fallen that afternoon, and in the sparkling air of that winter night just before Christmas, he was mesmerized by the simple beauty of twinkling starlight shining through a small fir tree, close to the place that housed his family. They were all snuggled in their beds and fast asleep. He couldn't wake them and compel them to brave the chill, to come outside and share in the beauty of the moment. He felt blessed, but lonely. He needed to share the glory of that moment.

Then it came to him. Why not take the starlight with him into the house, or at least a reasonable facsimile. Their Christmas tree was already in place in the living room. He stripped off the decorations that were already in place on the boughs, and he found enough candles to fill the branches. Lighting those tapers, he stepped back and admired their glow. Then he quietly organized his little family and marched them into the tree room where they all stood in awe, looking at the first lighted Christmas tree.

That happened over 400 years ago. You would remember that man as the leader of the Protestant Reformation, but his family knew him as the man who started the tradition of lighting the Christmas tree—Martin Luther.

THE WONDER of CHRISTMAS Is GIVING

# SANTA'S CHRISTMAS EVE PRAYER

The sleigh was all packed, the reindeer were fed,
But Santa still knelt by the side of the bed.
"Dear Father," he prayed, "be with me tonight,
There's much work to do and my schedule is tight.

"I must jump in my sled and streak through the sky,
Knowing full well that a reindeer can't fly;
I will visit each household before the first light,
I'll cover the world and all in one night.

"With sleigh bells ringing I'll land on each roof,
Amid the soft clatter of each little hoof.
To get in the house is the difficult part,
So I'll slide down the chimney of each child's heart.

"My sack will hold toys to grant all their wishes,
The supply will be endless like the loaves and the fishes;
I will fill all the stockings and not leave a track,
I'll eat every cookie that is left for my snack.

"I can do all these things, Lord, only through You.
I just need Your blessing, then it's easy to do.
All this to honor the birth of the One
That was sent to redeem us, Your most Holy Son.

"So to all of my friends, lest Your glory I rob,
Please, Lord, remind them who gave me this job."

# THE GUEST

Conrad was a godly old shoemaker, who one night dreamt that Christ would come to his shop on the following day. Early the next morning he went out to the woods to gather green boughs to decorate his shop for the Lord's coming.

All morning Conrad waited, but the only visitor who came by was an old man. He asked if he might sit down to rest. Conrad saw that the visitor's shoes were very worn, so before sending the stranger on his way, Conrad put the best pair of shoes in the shop on the man's feet.

Throughout the afternoon he waited for the Lord's coming, but the only person he saw was an old woman, who struggled under a heavy load. Out of compassion he brought her in and gave her some of the food he'd prepared for Christ. She went on her way refreshed, and the shoemaker continued his vigil.

Just as the shades of night were falling, a lost child entered his shop. Conrad took the child home and then hurried back so he wouldn't miss the coming of Christ.

He waited long with patience; Jesus did not come. Finally, in great despair, the old shoemaker cried:

"Why is it, Lord, that Your feet delay?
Did You forget that this was the day?"
Then soft in the silence, he heard a voice saying,
"Lift up your heart. I kept My word.
Three times I came to your friendly door,

And three times My shadow was on your floor.
I was the beggar with bruised feet.
I was the woman you gave food to eat.
I was the child of the homeless street.
I was all of these.
When you have done it to the least of these, you have done it unto Me...

"And I thank you."

And Conrad, through grateful tears, replied, "And I thank You."

# IF WE HAD NEEDED

The Christmas story is serenely simple—
- as effortless as a silent dawn.
- as unbelabored as a bursting rose.
- as natural as a baby's cry.

God wanted this gesture of love understood by all men—
- no flaming chariot bore Him down from heaven.
- no mighty cannonade announced His appearing.
- no bugles to fanfare His birth.
- no cadence of marching armies.
- none of the grandeur we would devise for so remarkable an event.

God's hand reached out and pulled down the dark curtain of night because He knew that in the darkness light always shines brightest.

And the joyful glow of the Christmas Star came—
- to Bethlehem telling us that no place is unknown to God;
- to Mary to convince us that no place is unknown to God;
- in a child declaring that all of life is in His hand;
- at the stroke of twelve to remind us that there is no moment of day or night when He is absent from us.

If we had needed knowledge,
>He would have sent us an educator.
If we had needed health,
>He would have sent us a doctor.
If we had needed wisdom,
>He would have sent us a philosopher.
If we had needed harmony,
>He would have sent us a musician.
If we had needed wealth,
>He would have sent us an economist.
 If we had needed success,
>He would have sent us an efficiency expert.
But we needed a Saviour
So He sent us Jesus.

And His name will be called
Wonderful,
Counselor,
Mighty God,
Everlasting Father,
Prince of Peace.

Isaiah 9:6 NKJV

# GOD DID!

*For God so loved the world, that he gave*
*his only begotten Son,*
*that whosoever believeth in him*
*should not perish, but have everlasting life.*

JOHN 3:16 KJV

Notice that God gave His Son—not lent—but gave.

Did you ever think of what that sacrifice meant to the Father? Knowingly He sent His only Son into a hostile world.

Many a mother experiences a portion of God's pain when she receives a telegram from the War Department stating that her own son has been killed in action.

Through her agony one mother cried, "I never knew giving a son could be so expensive!"

> If you had only one son,
>> would you send him to this earth
>> to live in lowly birth
>> where no one felt his worth?
>
> God did!

> If you had only one son,
>> would you let him leave his throne
>> and come to live unknown
>> and face his task alone?
>
> God did!

If you had only one son,
would you let him serve and bless
a crowd that offered less
than love and faithfulness?
God did!

If you had only one son,
would you let him weep and grieve
for men who won't perceive,
but only make believe?
God did!

If you had only one son,
would you let him pay sin's debt
for men who soon forget
and live without regret?
God did!

If you had only one son,
would you let him bleed and die
upon a cross held high
between the earth and sky?
God did!

If you had only one son,
　　　　would you raise him from the tomb
　　　　to lift away the gloom
　　　　from earth with still no room?
God did!

If you had only one son,
　　　　would you send him back again
　　　　to face a world of men
　　　　who still are lost in sin?
God will!

GOD WILL!

**GOD WILL!!!**

*The Light from heaven*
*came into the world.*

JOHN 3:19 TLB

# CHRISTMAS AT MY HOUSE

We had just finished opening our gifts when the whole truth dawned on me, and I finally felt, as well as understood, that my whole family had it—the spirit of Christmas. The five of us had spent the early morning hours sitting around the Christmas tree in our den. The fireplace was alive with a crackling blaze, and the tree was covered with a heterogeneous conglomeration of multicolored lights, ornaments, and tinsel that seemed to reach out with unorganized love.

We had all oohed and aahed for days about the packages resting promisingly under the branches. And on Christmas morning, we waited patiently while they were passed around by Santa's helpers. (Stephanie, Jeremiah, and Jaci were still doing that because I enjoy it so much.) Then we took turns opening gifts one at a time.

We were each appropriately excited about every present we received. I couldn't help but notice the extra light of joy in the eye of the giver as the givee squealed with happiness. I began to realize that a family is just about all grown up when they're more excited about giving than about getting.

I guess Jesus was right! That is the greatest lesson of Christmas. It really is "more blessed to give than to receive" (Acts 20:35).

That spirit of Christmas must keep on giving. It doesn't end in just one day. It's more than a season. It's a lifestyle!

When the song of the angels is stilled,
When the star in the sky is gone,
When the kings and princes are home,
When the shepherds are back with their flock,
Then the work of Christmas begins:
To find the lost,
To heal the broken,
To feed the hungry,
To release the prisoner,
To rebuild the nations,
To bring peace among brothers,
To make music in the heart.

Because Jesus came then,

Christmas is now.

# A BOX FULL OF KISSES

It was three days before Christmas, and Daddy was very busy wrapping presents. Six-year-old Katie stood at the table and asked Daddy for a box—a big box for a special Christmas present. He hardly glanced at her because he was so busy, but he did manage to pull a good-sized box from his wrapping pile.

"No," Katie said. "That's not big enough." She pointed and said, "I want the biggest box you have."

"Why do you want such a big box?"

"Because it's a very big surprise."

"Okay," Daddy muttered. "I hope this is important."

"Oh, it is," Katie replied. "But now I need some paper." Daddy reached for the least expensive roll—the tattered tissue used for stocking-stuffer gifts.

"Uh-uh," Katie insisted. "I need that pretty gold stuff."

"Uh-uh," Daddy replied. "That pretty gold stuff cost $15 a roll. The only reason we bought it was to help the little boy next door with his school fund-raiser."

"I don't care," Katie responded. "I want the nicest paper you have for this present. It's a very special, big surprise."

Daddy gave in mostly to get her out of his way. "But be careful," he cautioned. "Save me some of that gold paper. I need it too." There were still a lot of presents for him to wrap. He muttered under his breath that he'd never in his life paid $15 a roll for Christmas wrapping paper.

Katie disappeared into her room for almost three hours. When she returned to Daddy's table, she handed him her "biggest box," wrapped again and again in gold paper.

"Didn't save me any, did you?"

"No. I needed it all," Katie replied. "It's for you. Open it now, Daddy. Open it now."

"But it's not Christmas for three more days, Katie. Why open it now?"

"Because I'm too excited to wait. It's really special."

Daddy tried to gently peel off the expensive paper a corner at a time. Maybe he could salvage a little of it for future use. But it was impossible. *Katie used enough Scotch tape to repair the hull of the Titanic*, he thought.

Daddy tore away the expensive paper and opened the box. There was nothing in it.

"Katie," Daddy said, "why did you use this big box and all this fancy paper for a box that's empty?"

Katie said, "Oh, it's not empty, Daddy. I spent all afternoon blowing kisses into it for you. This box is full of how much I love you."

It is good to be
children sometimes,
and never better
than at Christmas,
when its mighty Founder
was a child Himself.

CHARLES DICKENS

# BETHLEHEM OF JUDEA

A little child,
A shining star;
A stable rude,
The door ajar.
Yet in that place
So crude, forlorn,
The hope of all
The world was born.

# The Wonder of Christmas Is ...

## ETERNAL

If you can't find Christmas in your heart,
you'll never find it under a tree.

# YES, VIRGINIA, THERE IS A JESUS

I t is truly heartwarming to know that millions of people around the world believe in Santa. Sure, most are under four feet tall, but still, it's amazing that so many believe in the big guy in the red suit. Consider the following:

Approximately two billion children (persons under 18) live around the globe today. Santa doesn't visit all of them, of course. Subtracting the number of Muslim, Hindu, Jewish, or Buddhist children reduces Santa's Christmas Eve workload to 15 percent of the total, or 378 million children (according to the Population Reference Bureau). At an average census rate of 3.5 children per household, and presuming that there is at least one good child in each home, Santa must visit about 108 million homes.

Santa has about 31 hours of Christmas to work with, thanks to the different time zones and the rotation of the earth and assuming he travels east to west, which seems logical. This works out to 967.7 visits per second. We can safely assume at each household with a good child, Santa has around 1/1000 of a second to park the sleigh, hop out, jump down the chimney, fill the stocking, distribute the remaining presents under the tree, eat whatever snacks have been left for him, get back up the chimney, jump into the sleigh, and move on to the next house.

For the purposes of our calculations, we will assume that each of these 108 million stops is evenly distributed around the earth (which, of course, we know to be false). We're talking about a trip of 0.78 miles per household—a total trip of 75.5 million miles, not counting bathroom stops or breaks. To cover that ground in 31 hours, Santa's sleigh moves at 650 miles per second, or 3,000 times the speed of sound. By comparison, the fastest man-made vehicle, the Ulysses space probe, moves at a poky 27.4 miles per second, and a conventional reindeer can run, at best, 15 miles per hour.

The payload of the sleigh adds another interesting element. Assuming that each child gets nothing more than a medium-sized Lego set (two pounds), the sleigh must carry over 500 thousand tons, not counting Santa himself. On land, a conventional reindeer can pull no more than 300 pounds. In air, even granting that the "flying" reindeer could pull 10 times the normal amount, the job can't be done with a mere eight or nine of them. Santa would need 360,000 of them.

This increases the payload, not counting the weight of the sleigh, another 54,000 tons, or roughly seven times the weight of the Queen Elizabeth (the ship, not the monarch).

Six hundred thousand tons traveling at 650 miles per second creates enormous air resistance. This would heat up the reindeer in the same fashion as a spacecraft reentering the earth's atmosphere. The lead pair of reindeer would absorb 14.3 quintillion joules of energy per second each. In short, they would burst into flames almost instantaneously, exposing the reindeer behind them and creating deafening sonic booms in their wake. The entire reindeer team would be vaporized within 4.26 thousandths of a second, or right about the time Santa reached the fifth house on his trip.

Not that it matters, however, since Santa, as a result of accelerating from a dead stop to 650 miles per second in .001 seconds, would be subjected to centrifugal forces of 17,500 g's. A 250-pound Santa (which seems ludicrously slim) would be pinned to the back of the sleigh by 4,315,015 pounds of force, instantly crushing his bones and organs and reducing him to a quivering blob of pink goo.

Considering all this, it's amazing that some children, and even a few adults, have no problem believing in Santa. By comparison, the story of the little baby born in the manger is relatively easy to believe. The life of Jesus Christ is a fact, recorded not only by biblical writers, but by secular historians as well, some of whom declare that there is more evidence for the birth, death, and resurrection of Christ, than there is evidence that Julius Caesar ever lived at all.

Jesus Christ is more than a myth. And He promises, to those willing to believe with childlike faith, an inheritance in the Kingdom of God.

WAYNE RICE

*"I am... the Bright
and Morning Star."*

REVELATION 22:16 NKJV

# THE TWELVE DAYS OF CHRISTMAS

Christmas is the season of the Christian year that begins on December 25th and lasts until January 6th, the Epiphany. That is when the church celebrates the revelation of Christ as the light of the world and recalls the journey of the Magi.

From 1558 until 1829, Roman Catholics in England were not allowed to practice their faith openly. During that era "The Twelve Days of Christmas" was written as a secret kind of catechism. The song has two levels of interpretation. The surface meaning, plus a hidden meaning known only to members of the church.

Each element in the carol is a code word for religious reality—

- The partridge in a pear tree is Jesus Christ.
- The two turtle doves are the Old and New Testaments.
- The three French hens stand for faith, hope, and love.
- The four calling birds are the four Gospels.
- The five golden rings recall the Torah, the first five books of the Old Testament.
- The six geese a-laying stand for the six days of creation.
- The seven swans a-swimming represent the sevenfold gifts of the Spirit.
- The eight maids a-milking are the eight beatitudes.
- The nine ladies dancing are the nine fruits of the Spirit.
- The ten lords a-leaping are the Ten Commandments.
- The eleven pipers piping stand for the eleven faithful disciples.
- The twelve drummers drumming symbolize the twelve points of belief in the Apostles Creed.

*F*rom all that dwell below the skies
Let the Creator's praise arise;
Let the Redeemer's name be sung
Through every land, but every tongue.
Eternal are thy mercies, Lord,
Eternal truth attends thy word;
Thy praise shall sound from shore to shore,
Till suns shall rise and set no more.

ISAAC WATTS

# WHEN YOU CAN'T SEE THE STAR

Every man could have seen the star and understood it, but only the wise men followed it. They were called wise because by profession and study they had mastered the lore of books and the wisdom of heaven. They were philosophers and astronomers, wise men who had accustomed themselves to look above the world of men for guidance and truth.

Now, there's no particular reason for limiting the number of wise men to three, except for the fact of three gifts: gold, frankincense, and myrrh. Early tradition says the kings traveled in a vast company, of which seven thousand were left at the Euphrates, while another one thousand continued on to Jerusalem.

Don't you know those kings of the East were objects of ridicule and scorn when they first announced that they planned to make a journey to a strange land to worship a new king by following a star? But aren't you glad their faith was stronger than their pride?

Did you know the wise men lost the star? That's right! Somewhere on their journey, the star disappeared. They had it well in sight when they began their trip. Actually, it was the appearance of that star that started them out across the desert to find the Son of God in the first place.

But they lost it! However, they kept going. They couldn't just park in the desert! And when they finally got to Jerusalem and entered Herod's palace, they didn't tell him where the baby was. Remember, it was only after conferring with his scholars that Herod told them that the baby was born in Bethlehem.

The wise men walked out of the palace, looked up, and there it was: "Lo, the star which they saw in the East" (KJV). Matthew 2:10 NKJV says, "When they saw the star, they rejoiced with exceedingly great joy."

What makes a star disappear? How would we ever lose it from sight? A heavenly vision-a holy calling. How could a star like that get lost?

Well, I suppose clouds could get in the way and block it from view. Or maybe the day gets too bright all around us. It's hard to see a star at noon! Sometimes we can become distracted. We tend to look at other things, and when we look back at the star, it's gone.

So what do you do when you can't see the star? Where do you go when you don't know where you are? What do you say when you can't find the way? Well, you keep going in the same direction you were going when you last saw the star. Like the wise men, you follow your dream of faith.

Just because the star is out of sight doesn't mean it's gone. It's still there to draw you closer to the Son of God.

God's hand reached out and pulled down
the dark curtain of night ...
because He knew that in the darkness
the light would shine the brightest.

And the star still shines,
making every Christmas
midnight clear.

# JUST SHEPHERDS

**S**heep intended for sacrifice in the temple at Jerusalem were pastured five miles away in the hills of Bethlehem. I was one of those simple shepherds caring for the flocks there, to whom the birth of Jesus was first announced.

Of all the people involved in the Nativity, we were the only ones who didn't have to travel to get to Christmas.

The angels had come from the other side of heaven.

The wise men journeyed from the other side of the world.

Joseph and Mary traveled from the other side of the country.

But the shepherds—we bowed at the manger, which was within the range of our voices. Christmas came to us.

Understand this: Shepherds were lowly people. We were at the bottom rung of the social ladder. No one was lower than tax collectors, prostitutes, and shepherds.

So, why should we be honored with God's Good News?

The people in Bethlehem were filled with the excitement of the visiting crowds at tax time.

The innkeeper was busy assigning rooms.

Herod was worried about a rival king.

The scribes and Pharisees were waiting for a Messiah to deliver them from the hated Romans.

Would these people care about a baby, wrapped in swaddling clothes, lying in a manger?

Not on your life!

So God passed up the "important" and spoke to the ordinary. He shared the news with those who would listen— just shepherds.

It was the eve of Christmas;
the snow lay deep and white.
I sat beside my window
and looked into the night.
I heard the church bells ringing,
I saw the bright stars shine
And childhood came again to
me with all its dreams divine.
Then as I listened to the bells
and watched the skies afar,
Out of the east majestic
there rose one radiant star.
And every other star grew pale
before that heavenly glow.
It seemed to bid me follow,
and I could not choose but go.

FREDERICK E. WEATHERLY

# I BELIEVE IN BETHLEHEM

I believe in a place called Bethlehem,
Where God's Son took human form;
I believe that the things which happened there
Still today can be reborn.

I believe the angels' song of peace
And good will toward men,
Can still be heard by those today
Who choose to hear again.

I believe that the star which pierced the night
Showing men to Bethlehem,
Is still reaching out to men of hope,
Brighter now than it was then.

I believe we must bow down
With shepherds once again;
And I still believe we all start there
At the town called Bethlehem.

I believe that the Babe grew up to die,
Gave His life all men to save;
I believe that He rose up from the dead,
Forever left an open grave!

I believe He'll come again,
The Conqueror over sin;
I believe He will find His room this time...
Let my heart be Bethlehem.

# THE LEGEND OF THE ROBIN

Long ago in a little village called Bethlehem, there was the beginning of a small family—a baby with his father and mother. They had come into the crowded town and could not find lodging, but a compassionate innkeeper allowed them to use his stable. That would provide a place off the street and out of the weather. At least the straw would be soft.

But in that makeshift shelter, the night air was very cold and the wind was raw. There was room for only a small fire which was unattended, and it provided no comfort for the newborn baby and his young mother. The father had gone to get some food for her, but she was left too tired to tend the flickering flame.

She spoke to the animals standing in the surrounding darkness. "Oxen, please, so this special child will come to no harm, get up and blow these embers warm with your breath." But the oxen were rapt in their sleep and did not stir.

"Donkey, will you blow on this flame?" But the donkey was dozing and didn't even hear her voice. And the horse, too, kept on dreaming beside his feeding box. The sheep were quiet in sleepy reverie, and even the dogs were silently drowsing.

Then suddenly the midnight stirred, and in from the cold there flew a brown bird on her way south. She saw the need for warmth and made a bellows of her wings, puffing her feathers into a fan. The bird was singing softly while the ashes began to glow and burn. Flames leaped out of the surging fire, but she kept beating with her quick little wings until all the stable was brought to warmth. And the baby slept softly cuddled in his mother's arms.

"Dear robin," the mother said, "from now on you shall wear that breast of red. Where the fire touched you, let that fire remain, a blessed and perpetual stain burned on your heart. Everyone shall always see that signature of charity."

# COLORS OF CHRISTMAS

White are the sheep that gather near,
Brought by men who seek good cheer;
White is the snow the cold wind blows,
White is the robe of swaddling clothes.

Yellow the star that shines so clear,
High above all our doubts and fear;
Yellow the star that calms our fright,
Brightest the star when darkest the night.

Green is the leaf of the tall palm tree,
Everybody down on bended knee;
Palm branches symbolize a King,
That is the song the angels sing.

Gold is the gift the wise men bring,
Golden riches for a King;
But kneeling down to worship there,
That is the gift beyond compare.

Night is blue and night is cold,
Mary's little Baby's only one day old;
Hush, little Baby, now don't you weep,
God made a promise He's gonna keep.

Red is the berry the holly grows,
Simple the meaning, everybody knows;
Red is the blood the Baby gave
When as a man He died to save.

Colors of Christmas are red and green,
White, gold, blue, and yellow, I mean;
These are the colors of Mary's Boy,
Born of God, bringing peace and joy.

✳

# THE FULLNESS OF TIME

Christmas did not happen by accident. It was carefully planned in the throne room of eternity, and on earth detailed preparation occurred for centuries. That's why the apostle Paul said, "When the fullness of time had come, God sent forth His Son" and the world was ready (Galatians 4:4).

The Hebrew people were unique in their worship of one God. The Greeks fashioned the most perfect language the world had ever known, and the Romans built the roads which connected the whole earth. Judaism was the mold which held the Good News. The Greek language was the vehicle to carry the Good News, and the Roman Empire was ready to spread the Good News.

So you see, Jesus came at the right time.

He came to a world of failure. The Jews were an unsatisfied people. The glory of Greece was past, and Roman rule was cruel and tyrannical. It was an unhappy, suspicious, fearful, needy world. It was a world filled with moral degradation, low ethical standards, bitter hatred, and unrelieved despair.

Sounds familiar, doesn't it?

But the coming of Jesus gave the world a fresh start.

That's why men have numbered their years from the date of His birth. That's when God's Son was given—not lent. God's Gift is outright. It has never been withdrawn. He is still here. Our emptiness invites God's abundance; our weakness cries out for His strength, and our blindness gropes for His light every day.

The fullness of time is still here.

And God hasn't changed. If you can't come to Bethlehem for Christmas, don't worry. Christmas will come to you.

The joyful glow of the Christmas Star came to Bethlehem
telling us that no place is too small for God to notice;
the holy light of the Christmas Star came to Mary
convincing us that no one is too insignificant for God to care;
and at the stroke of twelve to remind us that there is
no moment of day or night when He is absent from us.

# I DID THE BEST I COULD

Joseph and Mary were in a hurry when they reached Bethlehem. It had been a long 80-mile journey from Nazareth, and the time of Mary's delivery was at hand. It was logical that they would stop at my place of business. I am the innkeeper. Now mind you, I'm not the only inn-keeper in Bethlehem—just the one you remember. And I'm afraid you remember me for the wrong reason.

Oh, it's true I told him, "I don't have a room to rent you. No, not for any price. The whole town is full."

Joseph pleaded with me because his wife was ready to give birth at any minute. I'll never forget the insistent sound in his voice. It was almost like a prayer: "Please, do something to help us. Don't turn us away."

I told him, "I understand. Believe me, I understand your anxiety, and your wife's agony. My wife and I had a baby boy 6 months ago. So I do understand."

Joseph countered, "But your understanding doesn't help. We need a closet, a private corner, or just some place to be alone."

And right here is where you think I really blew it. You perceive me to be a hard-hearted businessman whose only concern was monetary advantage and profit. But you're wrong. I'd have done anything for that desperate couple as there was no place for them to go.

The crowds in town for the tax census had filled up every nook and cranny. People were already sleeping in the streets.

I'd have let them stay in our room, but it was already rented.

Here was my solution. We did have a stable at the inn. Not what you'd call grand accommodations, but it did get them off the street and out of the weather. I sent them in there. We took them blankets and water and made them as comfortable as possible.

My wife and I were right there when the baby Jesus made His entrance into this world. We were so happy for Joseph and Mary. Our hearts were overflowing with joy. Some shepherds came in from the fields where they had been watching their sheep. They said they had been sent by angels to find a baby wrapped in swaddling clothes—to this stable, at my inn.

Just think ... the hinge of history became a reality right where I lived. You're right. I didn't have much to offer, but I did what I could to welcome the newborn King.

This Christmas, I hope you do the same.

# ONE SOLITARY LIFE

Born in an obscure village, He was the child of a peasant woman. He grew up in yet another village, where He lived in poverty, was reared in anonymity, and worked in a carpenter shop until He was thirty.

Then for three years He was an itinerant preacher. He never wrote a book. He never held an office. He never had a family or owned a house. He didn't go to college. He never visited a big city. He never traveled two hundred miles from the place where He was born.

He did none of the things one usually associates with greatness. He had no credentials but His name. In birth He startled a king, in boyhood He puzzled the wise, in manhood He ruled the forces of nature.

He was only thirty-three when the tide of public opinion turned against Him. His friends ran away. He was turned over to His enemies and went through the mockery of a trial. He was nailed to a cross between two thieves. While He was dying, His executioners gambled for His clothing. And when He was dead, He was laid in a borrowed grave through the compassion of a friend.

Great men have come and gone. But He lives on. Herod could not kill Him, Satan could not seduce Him, death could not destroy Him, and the grave could not hold Him.

Twenty centuries have come and gone. Today He is the central figure of the human race and the leader of mankind's progress. Now, it is no exaggeration to say that all the armies that ever marched, all the navies that ever sailed, all the parliaments that ever sat, all the kings that ever reigned, put together, have not affected the life of man on this earth as much as that one solitary life.

*The true light that gives light
to every man was coming into the world.*

JOHN 1:9 NIV

# The Wonder of Christmas Is...

## REDEMPTION

The Son of God became the Son of Man,
so the sons of men might become
the sons of God.

# QUITE A LITTLE BABY

QUITE A LITTLE BABY IN THE HAY;
QUITE A LITTLE BABY BORN THAT DAY...
QUITE A LITTLE BABY, DON'T YOU SAY?
JESUS CHRIST, THE LORD.

With His hands He made the world and hung the moon and stars. He held the water and the land and then made them stand apart. Then with His hands He filled the sea with fish and living things. He painted leaves on all the trees and caused the birds to sing.
That's quite a little baby.
With His hands He made a man, who lived and breathed and stood, and as God looked at all He'd done, He whispered, "It is good!" But Satan came to war with God and caused the fall of man. Redemption came in human form that first Christmas night in Bethlehem.
That's quite a little baby in the hay.
But He didn't come just to be born. He came to live on earth, the perfect Son of man. He showed the world His Father's love with holy helping hands. He healed the sick and fed the poor, while His fame spread throughout the land. His name was loved,
and His work was known, because of His two hands.
That's quite a little baby born that day.

One day those in power came and took Him from His own.
They led Him to a rugged hill, where a cross would be His
throne.  He spoke of them with forgiving words: "Father,
forgive them; for they know not what they do."

That's quite a little baby, don't you say?

And finally, when they pierced His side, to prove
how much He still loved them all, He spread His hands out
wide. And died.

QUITE A LITTLE BABY IN THE HAY;
QUITE A LITTLE BABY BORN THAT DAY...
QUITE A LITTLE BABY, DON'T YOU SAY?
JESUS CHRIST, THE LORD

*This is a faithful saying, and worthy of all acceptation,*
*that Christ Jesus came into the world to save sinners;*
*of whom I am chief.*

I TIMOTHY 1:15 KJV

# CHRISTMAS AT BECKI'S HOUSE

Becki was four. She wanted to play that December afternoon, but Mother pushed her aside. "Becki, I'm just too busy today. There are presents to buy, cakes to bake, and rooms to clean. It's Christmastime, you know."

So Becki played alone.

When Daddy came home she rushed to the door with arms outstretched, ready for her usual hug and kiss. But Daddy's arms were already full of boxes and bags.

"Ooo ... for me?" she gasped.

"No ... for later. It's Christmas, you know. Run along now."

So Becki played alone.

At supper both Mommy and Daddy were so busy talking and planning the Christmas celebration, with Grandma and Grandpa and all the relatives coming over, that Becki couldn't get their attention. So she reached for the butter by herself. Somehow her elbow got all tangled up with her milk glass, and over it went.

"Oh, Becki ... not tonight," Mommy moaned. "Everyone is so busy. It's Christmastime! Run on to bed now. I'll be there in a minute to help you say your prayers."

She was already kneeling when Mommy walked in. Becki's prayer was simple—good for all of us. "God, forgive us our Christmases, as we forgive those who Christmas against us."

"Ready for Christmas," she said with a sigh.
As she gave a last touch to the gifts piled high.
Then wearily sat for a moment to read
Till soon, very soon, she was nodding her head.
Then quietly spoke a voice in her dream,
"Ready for Christmas, what do you mean?"
She woke with a start and a cry of despair.
"There's so little time and I've still to prepare,
Oh, Father! Forgive me, I see what You mean!
To be ready means more than a house swept clean.
Yes, more than the giving of gifts and a tree.
It's the heart swept clean that You want to see.
A heart that is free from bitterness and sin."
So be ready for Christmas ... and ready for Him.

# THE SON OF MAN

Jesus summed up the purpose of Christmas himself:
THE SON OF MAN IS COME
TO SEEK AND TO SAVE
THAT WHICH WAS LOST.
Eighty-three times He called himself "The Son of Man."
That was His favorite title. All other names turn out to be
words of limitation.
He could have been called the Son of Abraham,
but that's racially limiting.
Or the Son of David,
but that's officially limiting.
Or the Son of Mary,
but that's a family limitation.
Those titles are all good.
But their weakness lies in their littleness.
They're exclusive, rather than inclusive.
Confucius is a son of China.
Plato is a son of Greece.
Hugo, a son of France.
Hemingway, a son of America.
Shakespeare, a son of England.
But Christ—He is the Universal One—
the son of no tribe or nation or empire.
He is the Son of Man,
who by His own words
came to seek and to save
that which was lost.

*"What do you think? If a man owns a hundred sheep,
and one of them wanders away, will he not leave the ninety-nine
on the hills and go to look for the one that wandered off?
... In the same way your Father in heaven is not willing that
any of these little ones should be lost."*

MATTHEW 18:12,14 NIV

# A CHRISTMAS GIFT RETURNED

**B**en was nine years old and had always loved boats—ever since his dad had spent time in the Coast Guard Reserve. There wasn't much in life that he enjoyed more than going to the San Francisco Bay, standing by the Richmond Marina, and watching all the boats. Any boats, big or small—it didn't make any difference as long as they were out on the water.

You can imagine his utter joy and delight when his main Christmas present was a model kit for making his very own sailboat. All the other gifts were easily forgotten as he rapturously studied his new treasure.

He spent all his winter spare time building his pride-and-joy watercraft. It was a beautiful sight to behold with its polished white enamel hull, hand-formed, well-smoothed lead keel, and the bleached-sheets-turned-sails billowing in the wind.

"Spring had finally sprung," as his Grandpa said, and Ben finally got to go down to the big pond by the estuary. He would watch his boat head out across the cove, then he'd chase it to the other side, walk it back, and start her out again.

But on the third day of sailing, somehow she went astray. Contrary wind? Curious current? Ben never did know—but he knew he had lost her. He searched for the best part of the next week. Never could find her.

He cried himself to sleep more than one night because of

THE WONDER of CHRISTMAS Is REDEMPTION

loneliness and despair. What do you do when that which you love the most slides out of your life? Ben couldn't come up with an answer. He felt so betrayed.

Then walking past the small strip mall by the pond, he stopped to look in the toy shop. He knew he would never find another boat to love like his, but it wouldn't hurt to look at what might be available for some future day.

To his absolute amazement, there in the store window was his sailboat! It was easy to recognize—his markings were everywhere. Rushing inside the store he breathlessly told the shopkeeper that he wanted his boat back.

"Sorry," said the owner. "That boat is mine. I bought it from a man who found it last week. If you want it, you'll have to pay for it."

"Please hold on to the boat till I get back," he pleaded.

Ben raced home, gathered all his resources, and zipped back to the store. He didn't even try to bargin with the owner. That was his sailboat, and whatever the cost, it would be worth it to hold that boat again in his arms, to put it back into the water, and share happy days together. He plunked down the full asking price, picked up his ship, and walked out the door, saying, "Oh, little boat. Now you are twice mine. First I made you, then I bought you. Now, forever, you really do belong to me!"

That's the Christmas story at its very essence. Jesus Christ, the Creator of all creation, the Lord of all lords and the King of all kings, first made us—from a heart of love and careful purpose, He designed our destiny. And He saw that it was good, but it was not good for long. Sin rose up to vie against heaven for God's creation.

Just like Ben's sailboat, we drifted away, caught by some contrary wind or curious current. We left the care and compassion of the Savior and, like sheep, we went astray, each one to his own way.

Unwilling to leave us lost, He searched and searched until He found us—and then, with His own blood, He bought us back. So now we are twice His—because first He made us, and then He bought us.

✴

# THE BREAD OF LIFE

*T*he baker woman in her humble lodge,
Received the grain of wheat from God;
For nine whole months the grain she stored,
Behold the handmaid of the Lord.
Bake us the bread slowly, slowly;
Bake us the bread, for we must be fed.

The bakerwoman took the road which led
To Bethlehem, the house of bread;
To knead her bread she labored through the night,
And brought it forth about daylight.
Bake us the bread slowly, slowly;
Bake us the bread, for we must be fed.

She raised her bread for thirty years,
By the fire of her love and the salt of her tears;
By the warmth of her house, so tender and bright,
And the bread was gold and brown and white.
Bring us the bread quickly, quickly;
Bring us the bread, for we must be fed.

After thirty years the bread was done,
It was taken to town by her only Son,
The soft white bread to be given free
To the hungry people of Galilee.

Give us the bread gladly, gladly;
Give us the bread, for we must be fed.

For thirty coins the bread was sold
And a thousand teeth so coarse and cold
Jawed it to pieces on a Friday noon
When the sun turned black and red the moon.
Break us the bread sadly, sadly;
Break us the bread, for we must be fed.

But when she saw the bread so white,
That living bread she had made that night
Devoured as wolves might devour a sheep,
The bakerwoman began to weep.
Weep for the bread softly, softly;
Weep for the bread, for we must be fed.

But the bakerwoman's only Son
Appeared to His friends when three days were done;
On the road which to Emmaus led,
And they knew Him in the breaking of the bread.
Lift up your head higher, higher;
Lift up your head, for we have been fed.

# DOWN THE STAIRWAY OF STARS

Down the stairway of stars to be born in a stall,
Christ came down from heaven giving up all.
Leaving the palace of glory above,
He came to redeem, our souls to love.
From the scepter of power,
From the bright angel band,
From the crown lined with stars,
From the throne of that land;
Leaving the riches at infinite cost,
Christ our Redeemer, seeking the lost.

Up that Calvary road, Jesus walked all alone,
He suffered and died our sins to atone.
Then He rose from the tomb, and He lives evermore.
He conquered our foe to open life's door.
From the gloom and despair,
From the scorn of that hour,
From the bondage of death,
From the thrall of sin's power;
Your soul to free from sin's prison bars,
Jesus came down the stairway of stars.

# THE BORROWED MANGER

*And so it was, that, while [Joseph and Mary] were [in Bethlehem],*
*the days were accomplished that she should be delivered.*
*And she brought forth her firstborn son, and wrapped him*
*in swaddling clothes, and laid him in a manger.*

LUKE 2:6-7 KJV

Have you ever wondered why God allowed His Son to be born in a manger? He, who could have had the most that heaven and earth together could offer, settled instead for the least. So what can we learn about Jesus and why He came from that simple birth in a little manger?

First, it's fitting that the Lamb of God should be born surrounded with animals, many of whom were to be used in sacrifice.

Second, the manger made Him accessible. Shepherds hurrying to the stables did not have to flash identification cards to get by. Wise men didn't have to write for an interview or sit in a waiting room while their credentials were cleared by some Secret Service agent.

Third, the manger demonstrated His attitude of simplicity. Things were never important to Jesus. People were and still are.

He always moved toward them and into their lives. He chose to be born in that borrowed stable, away from everything comfortable and easy. Does that surprise you?

Later He said that when He slept, He had no bed. And He

borrowed a basket that bright spring morning before He sent the people away fully fed.

He borrowed a boat from which to preach His Father's love to the men who stood that day on Galilee's beach, wanting to hear His message again.

He borrowed a donkey on which to ride into Jerusalem. And he borrowed a room in which to meet His friends and have a last supper together.

He borrowed a table on which to eat, and the towel He used to dry His disciples' feet was not His own.

He borrowed a cross on which to die, and He even borrowed a tomb in which to lie. And yet the whole universe was His to enjoy.

Now He's looking for a life to share. It doesn't have to be regal, elegant, or fancy. In fact the plainer, the simpler—the better ... just an open heart into which He can move. Maybe yours.

# NO ROOM

We know there was no room for Jesus at the inn, but why? Who filled the six rooms in that Bethlehem hotel? Well, I don't know either, but let's suppose—

Room One is occupied by a man and his wife in their mid-forties. They're wealthy, big spenders. They have stopped in Bethlehem only to meet the Roman census requirements. Their room is filled with the pursuit of pleasure, with no regard for anyone or anything. They proved only that a person wrapped up in himself is a very small package.

Room Two is occupied by a fugitive running to escape arrest and punishment. There's a reward for this lawless man, and the innkeeper gives him a room only out of fear. First, you make your choices, then your choices make you.

Room Three is rented to a Roman soldier sent by the government to keep law and order in Bethlehem. He's official. He's pompous, demanding, and self-centered, confirming that people are like letters—those marked important seldom are.

Room Four belongs to a Pharisee of the Pharisees, proud of his orthodoxy and impressed with self-importance. He's critical, censorious, and always determined to convince others that he is in close alliance with God. He demonstrates clearly that a person can be straight as a rifle barrel, and just as empty.

Room Five is occupied by the innkeeper's cousin, a

wheeler-dealer, money-maker, and land-grabber. "If you're not making money, what's the point of living?" is his motto. He has a master's degree in greed and is living proof that nothing $ucceed$ like exce$$.

Room Six remains empty, reserved for the great guest who someday might come. Perhaps a Roman governor or philosopher, or maybe even the Messiah. The room, so full of empty dreams, leaves no room for Jesus. If you want your dreams to come true, first you must wake up!

What was the innkeeper's name? It could just as easily be yours or mine if we, too, crowd the Christ out of our lives. Remember, He still says, "I stand at the door and knock. If anyone hears my voice and opens the door, I will come in" (Revelation 3:20 NIV).

# MISSIONARY IN A MANGER

Jeffrey Bull, while a missionary to Tibet, was captured by the Chinese Communists. He was taken to a small house, where a Tibetan landlord had swept out an upstairs room for him.

When it was dark, Mr. Bull was ordered downstairs to give hay to the horses. He clambered down the notched tree trunk to the lower floor, which was given over to a stable. It was pitch black. His boots squished in the manure and straw on the floor. The stench of the animals was nauseating. He felt his way among the mules and horses, expecting to be kicked at any moment. What a place.

As he groped his way through the darkness, he asked himself, *What is today?* During travels since his capture, his mind had become muddled. Then it hit, *It's Christmas Eve ...* He stood still in that oriental manger, his mind reeling.

To think that the Savior was born in a place just like this. Jesus left heaven and came to this earth. He laid down His scepter of power in exchange for a piece of broken straw, clutched in a baby's hand. The angels sang one last "Hallelujah Chorus," but in the manger, all He heard was the lowing of cattle. All the host of heaven bowed down to worship Him, but in Bethlehem there were only a few shepherds.

Reminded of all that, Mr. Bull, with deep gratitude and new understanding, knelt in the mud and slime of that manger. And he sang...

"O come, all ye faithful, joyful and triumphant.
Come ye, o come ye to Bethlehem."

he Word became flesh...

The Master became servant...

The Creator became man...

The Perfect became sin so that old would become new...

Death became life...

Slave became heir...

Sorrow became joy...

So that we would be His forever.

# THE TALLEST TREE IN THE WORLD

Once upon a hill,
Three trees were standing tall;
Dreaming what they'd like to be,
If trees can dream at all.
One tree longed for palaces,
Another treasures rare,
The third tree chose to forever stand,
Pointing men to God.

More than anything, the first tree wanted to be part of a beautiful palace where one day a great king would dwell.  The second chose to be made into a large seaworthy ship, sailing all the oceans of the world with great treasure.  The third tree wanted to stay right where he was.  He dreamt of growing so high that whenever men saw him, he would cause their eyes to look to heaven, and then they'd think of God.  He wanted to be the tallest tree in the world.

Those trees shared their dreams for years.  Don't you know it was a happy day for the first tree when the axe cut him down, and he was carried into town.  But he wasn't made into a palace.  Instead, he became a feedbox for cattle and was thrown into a barnyard.  His dreams were gone.  No king would ever see him now.

The second tree fell to the axe and was thrilled when they took him to the shipyard. But, oh, the disappointment!  No beautiful ship to sail the oceans of the world would he become; instead, rough hands fashioned him into a fishing boat. No treasure here—just failure and loneliness.

The third tree tried to stop the woodsman, but the man wouldn't hear. He chopped the tree—cut him in two, and tossed him in back of the carpenter's shop to be forgotten. All he ever wanted to be was the tallest tree in the world.

Then one day God's love touched the little feedbox, and that first tree finally got his wish. He housed a King the night that Mary laid her baby in the manger.

The second tree—the lonely, smelly, fishing boat—his day came when a man was walking by the seashore. The crowds were so great, they were pushing him into the water. A fisherman spoke up, "Master! Use my boat for a pulpit. You'll be safe here." Jesus stepped into the boat, and the tree knew he was carrying the greatest treasure the world had ever known.

The third tree hated it when they took his two pieces and crossed them. He cried when they nailed that Man to him and lifted him up. All he had ever wanted to do was grow tall and point men to God. But today, every time we look at that tree, we always think of God, because He's the tallest tree in the world.

# A SONG ... A STAR ... A SON ...

A simple song,
A single star,
A special Son ...
God's only One.
A song that caroled peace on earth,
A star that told the Savior's birth;
A Son, God's gift of matchless worth
A song ... a star ... a Son ...

# WHEN DOES SOON BECOME NOW?

The national lament had gone on for over 400 years. The spiritual sky had turned gloomy and heavy, and no matter how hard and long the people prayed, God was not hearing.

The nation had been overrun by invading, godless armies. Temple worship had been disrupted and tarnished. Holy instruments of worship had been misused, corrupted, or destroyed. A dark cloud of despair hung over the countryside like a shroud at a funeral. The silence of God had become unbearable.

> "How long? How long?
> Emmanuel, how long?
> How long, O Lord, wilt Thou forget us?
> How long, O Lord, wilt Thou neglect us?
> Thy words, O Lord, they are true words;
> Thy words, O Lord, they are pure words.
> As silver tried in a furnace,
> Purified seven times.
> Thou hast promised a Redeemer,
> But when shall He visit His people?
> Some say His advent is soon...
> But when does soon become now?
> We know His name shall be called...
> Wonderful, Counsellor, Mighty God,
> Everlasting Father, and the Prince of Peace.

He shall be the Bread of Life, the Holy One,
King of kings, Lord of lords,
Lamb of God, Word of Life,
Rose of Sharon, Morning Star,
And Emmanuel ... God with us."
Suddenly, through the darkness there appeared the light of a
bright star and sound of angel voices...
"Rejoice! Rejoice!
Emmanuel has come to thee, O Israel."
And the nation prayed anew...
"O come, Emmanuel,
And ransom captive Israel,
That mourns in lonely exile here,
Until the Son of God appears."

# STARS IN THE WINDOW

During World War II, all across America banners were hung in the windows of homes where young men had gone off to the service. You remember, one blue star for each son who left, and a gold one if he wasn't coming home. One evening a young boy was walking down the street with his father. The stars and the banners caught his eye, and after a time, he began counting them.

"One star in that window," he announced. "And one in the next." He clapped his little hands and shouted out, "Oh, look, Daddy! There are three stars at that house." He ran up and down the avenue pointing out stars and pulling his daddy along.

Then they reached a house that puzzled him. "Look at that big house. It has lots of windows, but there's not one star—not even one. Why, Daddy?"

The father thought for a moment and then replied, "I guess they didn't have a son to give." Daddy was getting the feeling that his little boy was too young to understand the meaning of all those service stars anyway. After all, how does one explain to a five-year-old the loneliness, hopes, and fears on the other side of those stars in the windows?

Then they came to a vacant lot. There were no houses, and no windows in which to hang service banners. But in the distance was a stretch of sky where one evening star brightly glowed.

"Oh, look ... look!" the little boy exclaimed. "There's one

THE WONDER *of* CHRISTMAS

star in God's window. That means God gave a Son too."

Then, noticing the gold color of the star, he added, "Oh! That means His Son died."

But just as that star still glows tonight, He still lives on, shining through every faithful heart.

What star is this,
with beams so bright,
Which shames the sun's
less radiant light?
It shines to announce
a newborn King,
Glad tidings of our
God to bring.

# The Wonder of Christmas Is...

# GLORY

A thousand times in history a baby
has become a king, but only once in history
did a King become a baby.

# WHEN CHRISTMAS BEGAN

From the other side of time,
before the foundation of the world,
Jesus Christ always was ...

They called Him King of kings
and Lord of lords.
He was adored by seraphim,
worshipped by cherubim,
and served by angels.

He was the Second Person of the Trinity,
sharing in creation,
ruling the universe,
planning the destinies of the ages.

But one day, two thousand years ago,
He left the throne room of heaven,
stepped through the pearly gates
onto the red carpet of time,
walked down the stairway of stars,
and entered this world by a manger in Bethlehem ...
and everything changed.

There He held a scepter of power in His sovereign hand,
... here He clutched a broken piece of straw in a baby's fist.

There the heavenly choir had sung one last "Hallelujah
Chorus,"
... here all He heard was the lowing of a few cows.
There angels had bowed to worship Him,
... here a few confused shepherds stood and watched.
There He had been the center of attention and adoration.
... here no one even knew Him well enough to make
a reservation at the inn for His arrival.

# WHAT'S IN A NAME?

W e don't pay much attention to names today. They carry very little significance to us. They identify us, but they don't describe us. We can know a person's name without having the slightest idea what that individual is like.

But the Hebrews believed that the name was an important part of a personality. It spoke of character. If they heard someone's name, they knew what kind of person he was.

For instance, the name Jacob indicated that he was a devious person, a trickster who could not be trusted. Barak means lightning. He could strike anyone without warning. Deborah means bee ... you know, the insect. She could be as sweet as honey, but she never lost her sting.

In like manner, the name of a place described its outstanding feature. Carmel was a garden land; Gibeah was a hill; and Horeb was dry. If a Hebrew knew the name of the place, he knew what to expect when he got there.

So you can see that the name chosen for God's Son held great significance. It was so important that it was determined in the councils of heaven. And lest there be any doubt about it, it was revealed to both Joseph and Mary— separately.

Today there is no name in the world so widely known and honored. There is no name so often remembered, or so greatly loved. There is no name more precious to both young and old alike. It is the name that means deliverer, rescuer, Saviour, and angel-sent. "Call His name JESUS."

*Jesus* ...
The name that identifies Him with our humanity.
The One who came to save His people from their sins.

*Christ* ...
The name that declares Him to be God's anointed.
The One sent from heaven to seek and save
that which was lost.

*The Lord* ...
The name that proclaims His authority as the God-man.
The One who is above all.
Who came that we might have life ...
And have it more abundantly.

# MISTAKEN TRADITIONS

The wise men saw a star the shepherds missed.

And the shepherds heard angels the wise men never knew existed.

Mary pondered thoughts in her heart that were too deep for the shepherds.

And Simeon saw in Christ a sacred significance that even Mary didn't understand.

Today we have views of Christmas that are quite fabricated from tradition.

Nowhere in Scripture does it mention that there was a donkey for Mary to ride on.

And the angels didn't sing. Luke writes, "There was with the angel a multitude of the heavenly host praising God and saying: 'Glory to God in the highest!'" (Luke 2:13-14 NKJV). In fact, nowhere in the Bible does it ever say angels sing. But don't be disturbed. It doesn't say they don't sing, either.

And there's no record that there were three wise men. Undoubtedly there were many who traveled in that party, for safety's sake. They brought three gifts—gold, frankincense, and myrrh.

They didn't come to the manger at the inn; they came to a house, Matthew says.

And they didn't present their offerings to a baby, but to a young child.

Herod had all the children under two years old slain. That should give you some idea of how old Jesus was when the wise men arrived with their gifts.

I hope none of this news disappoints you, because none of these trappings are really important anyway. They're only bright ribbons on the package of God's gift.

Christmas must never degenerate into sentimentality. Our hearts must be moved to faith, and our wills to action. Nothing does us good, unless it makes us good.

And nothing makes us good, unless it makes us good for something.

*Come, kneel before the Lord*
*our Maker, for he is our God.*

PSALM 95:6-7 TLB

# AN ALLITERATED ADVENT

C   Our calendar calls, "COME CELEBRATE THE CHRIST CHILD." Candy, candles, carols, and concerts customarily characterize this commemoration. Christ is the center of our celebration.

H   We heed the harp heralding the highlight of history. The humble manger holding God's gift to humankind, as the heavenly hosts fill the heights of heaven.

R   Let's reflect in reverence as we remember the reality of the ringing reception, with the praises of the angels robed in righteousness, reverberating the radiance of the realm, rejoicing over our Redeemer.

I   The indescribable infant, Immanuel. The immaculate conception, the innkeeper, and the incarnation each illustrate important aspects of the incredible, irrefutable event.

S   The supernatural scene was set. The sky shone. Suddenly the shepherds out under the stars were summoned and sent to see the Savior, swaddled in soft simplicity. The shepherds returned to their sheep, sending praises to God for what they had seen.

T   No telephone, no telegrams, no television—just the tremendous truth told by those who traveled toward the tiny town of Bethlehem. There they were touched by the truth. Then they departed, giving thanks, and testifying to their theme, the things they had been told.

M   Our Messiah! What a monumental move He made from the majestic heavenly throne, to the modest atmosphere of the manger and a mattress of new-mown hay. The meaning of the magnificent, musical message echoed from the manger, as they awaited the Magi.

A   An abundance of adoring angels assembled to sing the angelic anthem, acclaiming, as the prophets had foretold ages ago, about the arrival of the infant. They admonished, "Don't be alarmed. We are here to affirm His birth." All were amazed.

THEN THEY ANNOUNCED...

S   The Savior! Our Savior! The Savior of all who surrender themselves to Him. It's that simple.

DON GRANT

# DON'T FORGET

This year we have invested two-and-a-half billion dollars in Christmas savings.

We will spend four hundred and fifty million on trees and decorations, three hundred and forty-five million for turkeys, and another twelve-and-a-half million for plum pudding.

Wait, there's more. One hundred million will be spent just to wrap the presents that people will hurry to exchange, and fifty-eight million will be spent for the fruitcakes that no one will eat.

And the federal government will put a billion dollars into circulation just to meet the demands of Christmas.

But do you ever get the feeling that we're missing the point of the celebration?

Examine this...

I have many friends. When they arranged to have a celebration in honor of My birthday, I was greatly pleased. Moreover, it was intimated to Me that preparations were being made for gifts to be given. This made Me happy, because I'm sharing My life with many people in great need, and in My present circumstances, I am wholly dependant on what My friends are doing.

Now, you may be sure that I looked forward to that day. And when it finally came, a vast number had remembered it, and My name was on every tongue. Gifts came in such profusion that I was overwhelmed.

But when I looked at the names of those to whom the gifts were given, I was amazed. Not one gift was for Me. My friends were giving gifts back and forth to one another in hectic complexity. I walked about enjoying the occasion as best I could, watching the happiness of others.

But what a lonesomeness I felt. I am the Christ, whose birthday people celebrate by giving gifts to each other, but not to Me. The gift I want most was best described by the apostle Paul when he wrote, "They first gave themselves."

*I am come that they might have life,*
*and that they might have it more abundantly.*

JOHN 10:10 KJV

# CHRISTMAS MEANS THE SAVIOR CAME

By Isaiah was foretold
What the shepherds did behold,
Jesus born in Bethlehem
Kin to God and Abraham.

Wise men came from far away,
With their gifts of great array;
And they gave Him everything,
Born a child and yet a King.

Angels sang of peace on earth,
All because of Jesus' birth;
Then they sang, "Good will toward men,"
Let's help sing that song again.

Christmas means the Savior came,
Hallelujah!
Jesus was His holy name,
Hallelujah!

# THE FAIREST FLOWER OF ALL

Many years ago just outside Mexico City, a Christian church established a beautiful custom of bringing to its sacred shrine at Christmastime great quantities of flowers. One year as hundreds of worshipers brought their tokens of remembrance of the birth of Jesus, eight-year-old Josephina stood beside the roadway and watched the people process into the cathedral.

At first, she wore an empty look of simple dismay, but that soon turned into quiet tears that made little rivulets, washing away some of the dust that had gathered on her cheeks. The people kept walking by, too busy in their celebration to notice a poor roadside waif.

Then her face fairly crumbled, and her tears overflowed in grief as she stood watching the townsfolk pass by with their arms full of blossoms. When the pastor of the church saw her, he paused and asked why she cried on such a joyous day. She sobbed out that she had no money to buy flowers to present to the Christ child ... and she so wanted to let Him know how much she loved Him too.

The resourceful priest bade her dry her tears and pluck the tall plant that was right at her side. She turned to look at it ... then protested, "It's a weed. I want flowers!"

"Pluck the weed!" commanded the priest. "Obedience is better than treasure."

Josephina shrugged uncertainly, but at his insistence she joined the parade to the sanctuary. The closer she walked to the church, the stem of the weed with the large green leaves began to glow with a soft red light. And when she placed her floral offering on the altar, it seemed to all who saw it to be the most beautiful gift of all.

Christ always recognizes the spirit with which the humblest worshiper brings a gift. The shepherds with their adoration were just as welcome at the manger as were the kings with their expensive offerings.

And from that day until now, it is said that the poinsettia plant has been the best-loved Christmas flower in that land where it now grows so plentifully ... a tribute to a little girl who wanted a special gift for the baby Jesus and learned that obedience is better than treasure.

✳

THE WONDER *of* CHRISTMAS *Is* GLORY

# THE BULLY AND THE BABY

Herod is really no stranger to the twentieth century. He is cut from the same cloth of tyranny as the dictators of our generation. He climbed the stepping-stones of bribery and butchery to the powerful position that finally corrupted him.

Herod became the governor of Galilee at the age of twenty-five. He so ingratiated himself with Anthony and Octavius that they appointed him king, and the Roman senate later conferred on him the full title, KING OF THE JEWS.

So you can imagine the absolute shock that overwhelmed Herod when the wise men appeared at his palace, inquiring where they could find the newborn King of the Jews. Herod blurted out the first thing that came to his mind: "Bring me word so that I may come and worship Him too!"

Herod, of course, had no intention of going to worship Him. He was just afraid that Jesus would threaten his kingdom. He never understood that the army Jesus would one day lead would be made up of volunteers whose only weapon would be love, and whose only cause would be peace.

Of all the people cast in the drama of the Nativity, only Herod did not go to Bethlehem. He stayed behind and became the man who missed Christmas.

And that could have been his glowing hour of great achievement. Had he laid his crown at the Child's feet, he would be highly honored today. As it is, his kingdom is now forgotten, and he is remembered as a dirty blot on the pages of history—as villainous as any man could possibly be.

But it is the Baby, grown to be Savior, of whom we still sing—King of kings and Lord of lords, forever and ever, hallelujah, HALLELUJAH, HALLELUJAH!

Christmas, my child,

is love in action.

Every time we give,

it's Christmas.

DALE EVANS ROGERS

# THE REAL CHRISTMAS STORY

And it came to pass in those days, that there went out a decree from Caesar Augustus, that all the world should be taxed. (And this taxing was first made when Cyrenius was governor of Syria.) And all went to be taxed, every one into his own city.

And Joseph also went up from Galilee, out of the city of Nazareth, into Judea, unto the city of David, which is called Bethlehem; (because he was of the house and lineage of David:) to be taxed with Mary his espoused wife, being great with child.

And so it was, that, while they were there, the days were accomplished that she should be delivered. And she brought forth her firstborn son, and wrapped him in swaddling clothes, and laid him in a manger; because there was no room for them in the inn.

And there were in the same country shepherds abiding in the field, keeping watch over their flock by night. And, lo, the angel of the Lord came upon them, and the glory of the Lord shone round about them: and they were sore afraid.

And the angel said unto them, Fear not: for, behold, I bring you good tidings of great joy, which shall be to all people. For unto you is born this day in the city of David a Saviour, which is Christ the Lord. And this shall be a sign unto you; Ye shall find the babe wrapped in swaddling clothes, lying in a manger.

And suddenly there was with the angel a multitude of the heavenly host praising God, and saying, Glory to God in the highest, and on earth peace, good will toward men.

And it came to pass, as the angels were gone away from them into heaven, the shepherds said one to another, Let us now go even unto Bethlehem and see this thing which is come to pass, which the Lord hath made known unto us.

And they came with haste, and found Mary, and Joseph, and the babe lying in a manger. And when they had seen it, they made known abroad the saying which was told them concerning this child. And all they that heard it wondered at those things which were told them by the shepherds.

But Mary kept all these things, and pondered them in her heart.

And the shepherds returned, glorifying and praising God for all the things that they had heard and seen, as it was told to them.

LUKE 2:1-20 KJV

# ABOUT THE AUTHOR

Derric Johnson epitomizes creativity and is renowned for excellence in talent and achievement as a motivational speaker, ordained pastor, prolific songwriter, musician, creative consultant, educator, and author.

He is a Stanley Foundation lecturer, featured in conferences and conventions nationally and internationally. Over the past 30 years he has served as a minister, authored ten books, written 150 original songs, 23 cantatas and 3,000 musical arrangements, published 32 books of choral collections, and produced 94 recorded albums on 12 labels.

He has been a specialty writer for Radio City Music Hall, and for 30 years he has served as a Creative Consultant for Walt Disney World, currently arranging, producing, and staffing Epcot Center's Voices of Liberty, America's premier a cappella stylists.

He currently resides in Winter Garden, Florida, with his wife, Debbie, and their daughter, Jaci.

Also available from Derric Johnson

*The Wonder of America*

Other Christmas books from Honor Books:

*Christmas Legends to Remember*

*Have Yourself a Merry Little Christmas*

*A Heartfelt Christmas*

If you have enjoyed this book,
or if it has impacted your life,
we would like to hear from you.

Please contact us at:

Honor Books, Dept. 201
4050 Lee Vance View
Colorado Springs, CO 80916
Or visit our Web site:
www.cookministries.com